Eve's Daughters

Miriam F. Polster

Eve's Daughters

The Forbidden
Heroism of Women

Jossey-Bass Publishers · San Francisco

For sales outside the United States, contact Maxwell Macmillan International Publishing Group, 866 Third Avenue, New York, New York 10022.

Manufactured in the United States of America.

The paper used in this book is acid-free and meets the State of California requirements for recycled paper (50 percent recycled waste, including 10 percent postconsumer waste), which are the strictest guidelines for recycled paper currently in use in the United States.

10% POST
CONSUMER
WASTE

Credits are on p. 207.

Library of Congress Cataloging-in-Publication Data

Polster, Miriam.
    Eve's daughters : the forbidden heroism of women / Miriam F. Polster. — 1st ed.
        p.   cm.—(The Jossey-Bass social and behavioral science series)
    Includes bibliographical references and index.
    ISBN 1-55542-464-3 (acid free)
    1. Women—Psychology. 2. Heroes—Psychology. 3. Heroines—Psychology. 4. Women—Socialization.   I. Title: Heroism of women. II. Series.
HQ1206.P58   1992
305.42—dc20   92-8806
                                                                   CIP

FIRST EDITION
HB Printing   10 9 8 7 6 5 4 3   *Code 9265*

The Jossey-Bass
Social and Behavioral Science Series

Contents

Preface

Many people today are lost in the day-to-day practicalities of their lives. One dimension of their dilemma is the confusion about the right way to be a man or a woman. The popularity of books, articles, lectures, and workshops on assertiveness in women and sensitivity in men—many of which link recurrent life themes to tales of ageless gods, goddesses, and heroes—reflects people's need to make sense of the rush of experience that threatens to engulf them. People feel like Alice in Wonderland, who finds herself, much to her dismay, swimming in a pool of her own tears.

Some people look to heroic examples, often culled from classic legends, for renewed perspective. Whereas these legends dramatize and personify heroic attitudes, psychotherapy must concern itself with the usefulness of these images in confronting personal struggles. As a therapist, I have observed that many people who come to my office are often so embedded in their disappointments or ashamed of their feelings of cowardice that nothing seems further from their possibilities than a call to heroism. Even so, they are often unknowingly governed by archaic stereotypes of heroism, outdated injunctions and condemnations that prevent them from bringing their own heroism to bear on their personal struggles.

Therapists know intimately about the heroism that occurs in commonplace settings with an unstellar cast of characters. The therapeutic relationship is rich with the opportunity to identify the heroic in a patient's life and then use it as a springboard for useful change. Recent studies demonstrating the importance of a practical and realistic sense of competence and hopefulness carry implications for therapy. The therapist may actually be the first person who offers a heroic perspective to a disheartened individual.

But this everyday heroism—a kind of microheroism—can be recognized in the lives of people who have never entered a therapist's office. *Eve's Daughters* is written for all women and men who presently balance personal aspiration against societal restrictions, either by themselves or in the company of others. Additionally, teachers and parents can use material presented here as a starting point when discussing personal heroism with their students and children.

There are two ways this book can contribute to such efforts. First, *Eve's Daughters* is a partial catalogue of the actual range of heroic behavior, which has provided inspiration over the ages. A varied and functional concept of heroism can still be a life-supporting influence for women and men surrounded by unrealistic and inappropriate images that discourage a sense of individual worth and achievement.

Second, the heroic legends we have inherited are so skewed to daring male adventures that they have obscured the heroism of women. Women and men have inherited a misleading, intimidating picture of what "real" heroes are like. Men are left with an uneasy sense that they are not heroic unless they conform to the classic mold. I describe a balanced concept of heroism that can help us modify standard masculine/feminine stereotypes and also reorient us to recognize undramatized and unheralded behavior as heroic.

The perspective on heroism proposed in this book underscores the value of a personal concept of heroism for women who work to make changes in their own lives and also in larger social arenas. Although vast social change is essential, the lugubrious pace of such efforts must not immobilize individual movement. Reform of the institutions and structures that might support an improvement in women's lives still lags far behind women's needs, the ones they confront every day. An empowering image of heroism will help women make changes in their own lives and may smoke out the institutions indifferent or inimical to women's welfare.

Organization of the Book

Eve's Daughters has three major focuses. The prologue and the first two chapters review the concept of heroism as it has evolved over centuries. The prologue contrasts the classic condemnation of Eve's villainy in the Garden of Eden with the universal admiration of Prometheus and points out how this double standard still influences our ideas about the "appropriate" heroism of women. In Chapter One, I review some of the historical definitions and examples of heroism that we have inherited. Basing my insights on legend, anthropology, and psychological research, I explore the different forms that heroism has taken, all of which either ignore women, simply find them convenient accessories, or admonish them anew against Eve's assertive example. In Chapter Two, I discuss some basic qualities shared by all heroes, women and men alike. In addition, Chapter Two suggests some elements that distinguish the heroism of women, giving it a unique character of its own.

The second focus addresses the differences in upbringing and expectation that affect the development—intellectual as well as behavioral—of boys and girls and the men and women they become. Chapters Three and Four scan the interaction between early physical and social conditions and the behaviors and aspirations of children, adolescents, and adults. Chapter Five expands this discussion by describing the long-standing ambivalence about women's knowledge or innocence. I argue that, although much heroic action is spontaneous, an informed interaction is usually a better springboard for heroism than naive confrontation.

The third perspective looks at the question of women's heroism based on patterns of exclusion and inclusion. Chapter Six reviews how women's status in their community relates to the community's economic conditions. Chapter Seven offers a map of the territories where women have traditionally been either unrepresented or almost invisible. Another environmental factor, explored in Chapter Eight, is women's relationship to their families, which differs from the classic male hero's pattern of relating to home and kin. Then Chapter Nine points out the ambivalent attitude toward women in their confrontations with human vulnerability, as they heroically tend to society's victims. Chapter Ten describes the world of the media, which, despite some progress, still wrongly differentiate appropriate behaviors and territories for women (thereby perpetuating a familiar and one-sided image of heroism).

Finally, in Chapter Eleven, I propose a concept of *neoheroism,* which joins with the emerging realistic heroism of women based on their effective use of knowledge and education. Women's unique attitude toward the use of power is recommended as a valuable correction for outdated adversarial habits.

Some Comments About Language

In this book I have used the term *woman hero* rather than *heroine.* To me, the word *heroine* has been used so often in literary analyses that it has come to be associated with fictional characters. Some of the women described are, of course, mythological. But the women of history and everyday life I described in this book are not fictions; they are all real. Furthermore, the word *hero* has such a compelling place in our hearts that it dwarfs other terms. I have never heard a woman say that another woman is her heroine. She says, "she's my hero." Incidentally, I have never heard a man refer to a woman as his hero (or heroine).

In addition, in order to protect the actual women and men to whom I refer in the book, I have changed their names and any features that might identify them. By whatever name I call them, though, they illustrate the pervasive relevance of the heroic to the unique and personal struggles in life.

Some distinctions need to be made here between heroes, mentors, and role models. All three influence human hopes and behaviors. But although there is some overlap between them, there are also some important differences.

The image of the *hero* arises from an outstanding act that is of such scope and benefit to others that people tell each other about it and repeat it beyond its original time and place to subsequent generations. As years pass, the story is embellished with each retelling until the hero becomes a legendary figure who may inspire extraordinary behaviors in ordinary people. In *Eve's Daughters,* as I have said, I want to remodel this image to restore it to human scale.

Unlike the hero, the *mentor* is someone whose influence is personal and immediate. Usually older or more experienced in a particular field or skill, the mentor may act as a guide, teacher, exemplar, or sponsor. The relationship assumes, either explicitly or implicitly, that the younger, less experienced person will be (for a time, at least) a student or an apprentice—or perhaps a disciple or protégé. The relationship is direct and works toward the maturation of the younger person into an important actor in a project shared by both people.

The *role model* may be either personally known or a distant figure one wants to resemble or, in some cases, replace. The influence of the role model may be indirect, for example, through biography or interview. But this relationship differs from the mentor relationship; if the role model is replaced, the successor usually wants to exceed her predecessor's work or put her own stamp on it.

For example, Barbara Harris, the first woman ordained as a bishop in the Episcopal church, could well serve as all three: role model, mentor, and hero. She may have inspired other women to aspire to that office; in that sense, she served as a role model. If she took other women under her wing and taught them what they needed to learn in order to be important in their churches, she was a mentor to those specific women. But if she inspired other women to speak out more forthrightly, to regard themselves as potent in religious or political argument, or to question and oppose unacceptable practices, she would be functioning as a hero.

Each of these three images is powerful and important, but the concept of the hero is especially rich. By leaving room for creative and personalized involvement, it moves beyond simple imitation or specific instruction. An individual is free to adapt the heroic example to fit her own experience and then to devise her own solution. This individual adaptability illustrates an important quality of heroism. A hero can affect one individual in a specific setting or be a grand image that may inspire multitudes. Nevertheless, a hero to one person or one million is still a hero.

More important, the heroic example implicitly transcends its specific action. It revives a timeless idealism that animates the individual spirit and breathes into it a persistent sense of hope and competence. Heroism is idealism in action. When women show us a previously denied range of heroic possibilities, a whole new continent of heroism is discovered—and we all, men and women, can become immigrants in a new land.

The perspective that enables a woman to reexamine her life is nourished by other individuals. The hero serves as an example. But others do it through recognition and encouragement. Therapists and friends must note the courage of their patients and companions. Teachers must celebrate the ingenuity of their students, and parents must nourish the bravery and persistence of their children. Hope can turn out to be a powerful motivator to live a fulfilling life.

A limited image of heroism, based on hand-me-down values, often discourages people from what they *could* do because it is not what they have been taught they *should* do. Stuck with untimely models, they are unable to conceive of currently useful behaviors. To counter defeating introjections takes courage because each individual must rework what she or he has been taught and construct a fresh, distinctive perspective on life.

Acknowledgments

Acknowledging the individuals who have helped me in the writing of this book is like saying good-byes: one is in danger of either saying too much or too little. I tend to err on the side of saying too little. Judith Bardwick listened thoughtfully on several occasions and shared with me a previously unpublished article. Herman Gadon and Natasha Josefowitz read and commented on my manuscript and have otherwise informed and encouraged me. I am grateful not only for the support of these good people but also for their friendship.

My special thanks to Nan Narboe, who commented wisely and wittily on the manuscript, recommended several books, and sent me wonderful poems. I want also to acknowledge the importance of Harriet-Carole Senturia, who daily confronted her life and death with a magnificent and heroic assertion of her own power to shape the manner of both.

Kathryn Conklin deserves my heartfelt thanks for her tireless help in preparing the final manuscript. Her shining face and buoyant spirit always made light of hard work.

To my editor at Jossey-Bass, Rebecca McGovern, go my thanks for her insightfulness and precision in the preparation of the manuscript. I shall always value the warmth and clarity of our interactions.

My daughter, Sarah, and my son, Adam, have patiently taught me (they are still teaching me) the facts of life. They, too, brought me books and sent me articles. They are dear to me for all of those reasons—and for many more.

And finally, my love and gratitude to my husband, Erv, whose sensitive comments and suggestions have been—in this endeavor as in many others over the years—a loving stimulus to do my best.

La Jolla, California   Miriam F. Polster
June 1992

The Author

Miriam F. Polster received her Bachelor of Music degree (1947) from Miami University and both her M.S. degree (1965) and Ph.D. degree (1967) from Case Western Reserve University in clinical psychology.

Polster is codirector of the Gestalt Training Center—San Diego and associate clinical professor in the Department of Psychiatry at the School of Medicine, University of California, San Diego. She has presented workshops in Gestalt therapy in the United States and abroad for the past twenty-five years. She is coauthor, with her husband, Erving, of *Gestalt Therapy Integrated* (1973) and has authored journal articles and chapters in several anthologies, including *The Evolution of Psychotherapy* (Zeig, 1992) and *Critical Incidents in Group Therapy* (Donigian and Malnati, 1987). She is also consulting editor of *International Journal of Group Psychotherapy* and serves on the editorial boards of several journals.

Eve's Daughters

Prologue

The message is clear: obey the rules and there's nothing to
fear from this God, this father.
— Lillian B. Rubin, *Women of a Certain Age*

Our images of heroism have their roots in some of the most trea-
sured stories and legends of Western civilization—the Greek and
Biblical stories of the creation of the first man and woman. The
stories of Prometheus and Eve illustrate the difference in the heroic
recognition given to men and women. Both Prometheus and Eve
disobeyed the explicit commands of their gods, but though their
behavior was strikingly similar, Prometheus is a hero while Eve is
regarded as a villain.

According to Greek legend, Prometheus made the first man,
kneading him from earth and water. Zeus, the lord of Mount Olym-
pus, further commissioned Prometheus to give gifts to all the creatures on earth—any gift but fire, which Zeus withheld for the
exclusive use of the gods. Like any proud father (but in this way
unlike the patriarchal God of the Old Testament), Prometheus
wanted to enhance the competence of the creature he had made.
After all, he had formed man to walk nobly upright in order to
better view the stars, so he wanted to give man something extraordinary to establish him even more firmly in dominion over the other
animals.

Since Zeus had declared that fire was to be used only by the
gods, what could be more special? So Prometheus defied Zeus, stole

1

the divine fire, and gave it to man. For this act of hubris he was chained to a rock, and a vulture came daily to nibble at his liver, which grew back again each night to prolong his torment. Prometheus gave humankind his great gift at considerable pain to himself. For this act, he has become a heroic figure, inspiring poets, playwrights, musicians, and painters. In all of his artistic manifestations he consistently appears as a noble figure.

By giving the first man the gift of fire, Prometheus provided him with a sense of entitlement that exceeded the mortal limitations that had been divinely ordained. His theft of fire from the gods transgressed the established boundary between sacred privilege and human possibility.

In the legend of Prometheus's heroic generosity, fire is a metaphor for the expansion of the boundaries of ordinary human action and possibility. Prometheus provided a divine resource for everyday use and asserted a proud connection between humanity and the highest level of spirit, vision, and capacity. In his play *Prometheus Bound*, Aeschylus makes this clear when he has Prometheus say that mankind lived like children "until I gave them understanding and a portion of reason" (Oates and Murphy, 1944, p. 150).

Eve, on the other hand, was beguiled by the serpent into eating the fruit of the forbidden tree. Since Eve and Adam could eat from *any* of the trees in the garden, there had to be something special indeed about *this* one. And what was it the serpent assured her that this tree could offer? "In the day ye eat thereof, then your eyes shall be opened and ye shall be as God, knowing good and evil." Once again an ordinary human is encouraged to aspire to a gift explicitly prohibited by the ruling divinity; however, this time the impetus comes from a disreputable source, unlike the legend of Prometheus.

Adam had told Eve that if they even *touched* the tree they would die. The wily serpent nudged Eve against the tree and then pointed out that even though she had touched it, she hadn't died. So, she might also be able to *eat* the fruit of the tree and not die (Graves and Patai, 1966).

Like Prometheus, Eve went against her god's explicit prohibition and claimed access to a privilege that was specifically forbidden. Eve decided, as did Prometheus, that a divine privilege might also be appropriate for human use. And she too, like Prometheus, was severely punished for her defiance. But with such different consequences!

Prometheus typifies a noble and classic "manliness" in his solitary sufferings. He is open; he doesn't lie or try to conceal his transgression. Eve, on the other hand, is portrayed as evasive and unadmirable. She has been blamed for all the evils that subsequently plagued later innocent generations, and her willful loss of innocence stained the rest of us. Tertullian, the early convert to Christianity, railed at Christian women: "Do you not know that every one of you is Eve?" (Pagels, 1988, p. 63). As one woman in seventeenth-century England confessed, "we of the weaker sex, have hereditary evil from our Grandmother Eve" (Fraser, 1984, p. 247). Very different indeed from the gratitude accorded to Prometheus.

Eve's punishment, unlike that of the noble Prometheus, was like the censuring of a naughty child. She was sent out of the room, her privileges were revoked, and all the other naughty children like her (women, that is) would forever share in her disgrace and in the punishment of bringing forth their children in pain. Adam would thereafter be required to provide his own food by the sweat of his brow. Her punishment, which was even more crippling, permanently tainted her relationships—with her spouse, who had to live with her in a world that was harsh and begrudging of food, and with her children, between whom jealousy and competition led to murder.

But take another look. Eve's action marked a maturation into a level of functioning more befitting thoughtful adults. Even her punishment of bearing her children in pain can be seen as an "objective account of the responsibility resulting from her new awareness" (Ochs, 1977, p. 20). Her act challenged all of us to move from a stage of infantilization, as children of a benevolent father, into mature responsibility and competence.

Eve's act of willful disobedience admitted her (and all of us, happily or not) into the forbidden world of the knowledge of good and evil, a world where personal judgment and responsibility replace docile obedience. Eve's unwillingness to live under restriction grew naturally from her liveliness of mind. She, like Prometheus,

had a curiosity that distinguished her from less-complicated creatures, animals for whom knowledge and choice were dominated by
immediate, practical need and controlled, therefore, almost exclusively by instinct. The knowledge of good and evil, like the possession of fire, requires the need to develop judgment, deliberation,
and conscience.

Most parents welcome the development of judgment and curiosity in their children because this accompanies their evolution
into intelligent and reasonable creatures. Eve marks the growth
from childhood through adolescence to adulthood. The myths of
Eve and Prometheus hint at the stage of human evolution where
primitive people may have begun to reject the unsatisfactory magical and superstitious explanations of their world. In the same way
adolescents reframe their relationships to their parents, these early
humans began to contemplate a god who did not have exclusive
rights to all the powers of the world.

At the heart of the Promethean legend is Prometheus's conviction that humankind had a right to divine fire—along with his
wish that fire be used wisely. Prometheus's gift was double-edged.
First, fire empowered otherwise helpless people by giving them
some control over their circumstances: to bring light and heat into
darkness and cold, for example, and to master clay, metal, and
animal products, shaping them to their own purposes.

But the implicit challenge of Prometheus's gift was that humankind had to develop an ethical and personal consciousness to
govern the use of this power. The legacy of Prometheus is obviously
still with us. Our nuclear abilities have escalated the simple "fire
power" of our early ancestors; the issue now is the development of
the wisdom and capacity to control those potentially destructive
forces.

The legacy of Eve is also still with us. She was unwilling to
live in a paradise where she had no control over her own thoughts
and behavior. Her example is reflected throughout history in other
revolutionary demands for self-government; the American colonists
said the same thing centuries later—there can be no government
except by consent of the governed.

Men in revolutionary movements (especially successful ones)
are often seen as admirable rebels. Like Prometheus, they are de-

picted as enlarging the self-determination and power of their countrymen. But when the suffragists, Eve's daughters, protested their
disenfranchisement and demanded a voice in the decisions made
about their lives and the lives of their children, they were seen as
demanding too much and (even worse) not behaving like the ladies
they were reared to be. Like Eve, they refused to restrict their intelligence and judgment to the realm of domesticity. Like Eve, they
were also claiming the right of women to learn what they needed
to know in order to wisely participate in their own governance.
They asserted that behaviors considered the natural prerogative of
men were equally natural for women. For many years they were
perceived as radical and impudent, not knowing their place—just
like Eve.

I remember one woman's account of her first day in graduate
school. None of Doris's family had ever even attended college, let
alone earned an advanced degree. Here she was, already an exception and daring to go even farther. Her mother viewed the process
darkly; this education would make her daughter even more different
from the rest of the family, and who knew if any man would want
to marry such a woman? Doris described driving to her first class
over a road with asphalt seams in between the road's segments.
"The car went bump, bump, bump down the hill, and I could feel
my heart going bump, bump, bump right along with it!" Doris
extended the limits of her own personal vision, like Prometheus, by
daring to claim an education exceeding what she had been told was
right for her, like Eve.

Conclusion

Men are primarily the heirs of Prometheus, not of Adam. They still
play with fire and take this as their rightful activity.

Eve, on the other hand, remains fixed in the sacred literature
as an unholy influence. Women are to take the simple innocence of
Eve as their ideal and shun the knowledge that Eve and her daughters paid for.

Eve's dilemma is reflected in the predicament that many
modern women confront. Hungry for the full exercise of their mental energy, they ask disturbing questions and make troublesome

demands. Many of these lively minded women encounter only opposition and punishment. Nevertheless, like Eve, their actions lead women out of a distant and lost paradise into a real world of pain, more struggle—and the possibilities of achievement.

The intelligence and knowledge that each woman must exercise in such self-determination, however, have been worrisome characteristics to men. Knowledgeable women have sometimes been welcomed—and sometimes not. Even so, few of them want to return to a state of imposed innocence. That is Eve's legacy: the assertion that it is the birthright of energetic, hardworking women to earn, by their own efforts, the right to make informed decisions about the conduct of their own lives.

A complete picture of heroism has to include the courage of both Prometheus *and* Eve. Women and men hunger for a *balanced* sense of heroic possibilities that draws from the best qualities of both.

ONE

The Heroic Legacy

The myth of Eve is neither unintelligible nor irrelevant . . .
Eve is very much alive, and every member of Western society
is affected by her story.
　　　　　—John A. Phillips, *Eve: The History of an*
　　　　　Idea

Newborn ducklings, monkeys, and other infant animals form instinctive, immediate attachments to their mothers, following them around devotedly. This built-in behavior guarantees their survival. Human children bond to their parents, too, imprinted in their own way. But soon parents are not enough; our original idolatry of our parents expands to a compelling interest in heroes of fact or fiction. Children look for heroes in gods, saints, and martyrs of our religious faiths; in fairy tales; in stories of famous combats; on athletic fields; in rugged and dangerous terrain; and in the outer regions of space.

As adults we look further: to cultural and media heroes; to people who show physical or mental courage, originality, and integrity; and to intrepid people who take risks and emerge triumphant. Hero tales full of suspense and drama captivate us from childhood to adulthood. Current literature argues that our response to heroism is one of our most compelling impulses (Becker, 1973; Campbell, 1988; Gerzon, 1982). Our need for heroes seems necessary for survival, although not as critical as our need for food, water, and air.

Nevertheless, the hero tales we have inherited are injuriously skewed. The classic heroes are usually male, and both they and their female associates have carefully stipulated roles to play. This slant is neither accidental nor the machinations of evil men out to ensure privilege for themselves. Then—as now—there were good reasons for heroic deeds, for example, the protection of loved ones or the defense of a cherished principle. Crises of survival (common stimuli for heroic action) may sometimes cancel out the more benign generosities of spirit such as sharing assets and skills or the graceful honoring of relationships. But we need to restore a *balance* between the familiar male virtues that have been honored in our concepts of heroism and the female virtues that have been overlooked in favor of flamboyant action.

This imbalance in heroic models has two damaging consequences. First, their actions are intimidatingly out of human scale, ill-fitting and unrealistic given the requirements of our modern age. Second, bad as they are for men, these male-skewed images have also stunted women's recognition of their own heroism. Yet in spite of being anachronistic, the old heroic images are still in place, albeit in "new and improved" versions, with modern packaging.

In fact, not only are we still recycling the old invincible models of male heroism, we have actually upped the ante. The ancient Greeks created an inaccessible image of heroes, for example, Achilles was part divine and part human—a great leap beyond ordinary humans. But Superman, with his exclusive mineral rights to kryptonite, is even more inaccessible than Achilles. What we really need are heroes who, even though they stretch our limits, are human scale. We need to gear ourselves to heroes whose lives can resonate to and *amplify* our own possibilities.

The ancient hero tale had shortcomings other than magnifying the hero beyond human scale. Primitive times, when much of our heroic legacy originated, had great need of aggressive, aggrandizing heroes who were bold, strong, fast, and physically direct. In those pitiless times, such characteristics were so crucial to basic survival that they became the undisputed hallmarks of the hero and ended up an indelible part of our heroic composite.

The predominant image of heroism immortalized for centuries has been action oriented. Boys and men are still admired for this kind of behavior. They are encouraged both by instruction and implicit messages to be tough, aggressive, and self-confident, whether or not this actually *fits* them or the times in which they live. The wounds of the glory period were also inflicted on women, even though they were merely accessory figures. Eventually these two images coalesced to form culturally endorsed standards of independent action for men and dependent passivity for women. Heroism came to be considered an exclusively masculine characteristic and one to which only certain men could aspire. Women occasionally were "heroic" (often to their eventual regret) but only if they emulated men. This image of heroism became a grand societal introjection, a massive "should" system.

Our image of heroism has women trying to live up to unfit and outdated standards. The same is true for men. This dilemma is only too familiar in psychotherapy, where much pain is traced to conformity with familial or societal images that fit the individual either badly or not at all.

What's in a Name?

"What's in a name?" Shakespeare's Juliet asks. Recognition, dignity, inspiration, and permanence, among other things. And all these are withheld when women heroes are deprived of their proper title. The courage and durability of women continue to be taken merely as women's fitting contribution, supporting the "truly" heroic actions of men and not worthy of separate celebration. Women's quiet but profoundly courageous acts simply go unremarked, submerged in a subsidiary world of attachment and service. When a heroic act is called by its proper and respectful title, it grows weightier. Simple actions are endowed with dignity and significance. Knowing who or what is heroic reinforces the human resonance to greatness; it also nourishes the greatness in our own lives by providing a sense of the diverse forms that heroism takes.

When we learn the word *hero* as children, we arrive fairly quickly at a good working sense of what it means. It conjures up the image of a person of spirit, of physical and mental courage, of integrity and farsightedness. The word evokes a bold individual who ventures into new and risky territory and does wondrous deeds there. We resound early to the word's significance, operating from almost reflexive, built-in connections that program us to respond.

This innate response to courage and nobility of spirit was—and still is—as important a reflex as other traits more clearly governed by instinct.

My experience with my grandmother was a miniature version of the timeless human response to heroism. She was my introduction to knowledge, enterprise, and mastery—and to mortality and immortality. I thirsted for the mystery and the extension of experience that she personified, and she, in turn, was generous with time, example, and attention.

Like many of yours, my grandmother came from a strange country. She had crossed an ocean; she sang songs and spoke a language that pointed to a world and a time that I didn't know. She carried in her tiny body a condensed history and geography that stretched beyond the flat pink, blue, and green maps that the teacher rolled down in my schoolroom. She taught me how to make things that were useful and beautiful. She initiated me into the great mystery of dying. In my childhood, she was one of my heroes. As an adult, I still find her heroic.

She knew well what major tragedies were. She had seen the death of several of her children. She had given birth to her last child, my mother, after her husband had died of a gangrenous infection when he refused to have his leg amputated. She had courageously uprooted her family and gone to an unknown country that offered no guarantees and only the slimmest of welcomes. She knew what small tragedies felt like, and she did not belittle them.

She taught me how to knit. Left-handed, I couldn't learn the right way and improvised a clumsy but workable style of my own. So fascinated was I with the transformation of a stringy piece of yarn into fabric and with myself as the medium that I simply took the process on its own terms, unaware of my grotesque technique. So did my grandmother. She knew I was moving into unfamiliar territory, and she supported my venture on its own terms.

I remember her looking at my knitting and smiling. She, whose needlework was perfect and exquisite, could understand and see it as I did, and she shared the ageless joy of creation. This was not a condescending response. She knew what excellence was and communicated her love of fine work to me. She knew, though, how long it took to get to that stage, and she figured we both had a lot of time. Hers behind her, knowing what it was like to learn, and mine ahead of me, getting better at what I was doing if I just kept at it and didn't get prematurely discouraged.

She died where she had lived, in my childhood home. Her death was foreseen and expected. Her daughters were there, and one of them began to weep noisily. It was early morning; my brother and I were already at school, but Grandma didn't know this. "Quiet," she said to her noisy daughter. "Quiet, the children are sleeping."

By the time I came home for lunch, the house was busy and full of women. One aunt, weeping loudly and with a sense of melodrama, beckoned me to my dead grandmother's bedside, tearfully exhorting me to kiss her for a last goodbye. I did. My mother, who had just heard of this in the kitchen, was very angry at what she feared would be a traumatic experience for me and drew me away.

My mother was mistaken.

My grandmother had never frightened me while alive, and lying there, so softly, sweetly dead, she still did not frighten me. She had always hinted at immense journeys and here she was, embarked on one of the greatest. She absorbed my last kiss as an acknowledgment of what she was in my life. And I knew that it was fitting to have kissed her.

I have a dreamlike fantasy about my grandmother. It began right after she died, and although I now have a grown-up's understanding, it is a connection to her that I will keep as long as I keep memory. The night of her funeral I went out onto our front porch and looked at the sky. It was early evening, and in the dusky sky was a solitary star. There it shone, so sweetly, coldly luminous, twinkling a little, but on the whole resting gently in its bed of sky. For me that first star of evening became my grandmother. I could not let the event of her disappear from my world. Though she was distant and unreachable, she still had an eye on me—and I could still see her.

Years later, when I began reading Homer, I learned that the Greeks, too, had made stars out of their heroes—Hercules, Orion, Perseus—and I recognized the shared impulse to immortalize our idols. Centuries afterward, there I was, innocent kin to the ancients.

Heroes: The Old Story

Heroic legends and stories have provided us with example and inspiration for centuries. Hero tales set forth, in dramatic and colorful terms, the cultural necessities of their day and provide us with models of how to survive hardships and challenges effectively. The conditions underlying the creation of heroic legends show that these legends were specific and appropriate to their times. They honored the economic and social necessities within developing civilizations and determined the most productive distribution of duties. Legends communicated the specific requirements for women and men, and the heroic image reflected the hierarchical assignment of community tasks. The prehistoric cave paintings depict a hunt, for example, showing that all the hunters are men. There is no accompanying portrait, however, of women at their tasks.

Women Heroes in the Old World: Absent or Overlooked?

Women's place in a masculine hierarchy would have to be complementary to the prominent heroism of men. And so it was. The women in ancient myths supported men's endeavors; they were helpers, victims, betrayers, or prizes.

Eventually "appropriate" roles for women and men developed: independence for men and dependency for women. These differing requirements defined what male heroism could be and virtually crippled the heroic possibilities for women. Furthermore, there developed certain settings where standard heroic action *could* occur. The hunt and eventually the battlefield were arenas from which women (with notable and usually troublesome exceptions) were excluded.

By contrast, the domestic scene, to which women were typically confined, was given low status. Home was seen merely as an incubator for future soldiers, an obscure setting in which nothing resembling heroism took place; so none was recorded. Domesticity dictated the predominately female settings where women were to focus their efforts and thus ensured that women's heroism was overlooked in the routine of daily life. The seventeenth-century French philosopher Malebranche voiced a widely held belief when he observed that a woman was better off safe at home because the delicate fibers of her brain disqualified her from profound thinking (Anderson and Zinsser, 1988b).

What was even more debasing than the undervaluing of women's contributions was the exclusion of women from other arenas. For centuries women were denied functional participation even in nonbelligerent settings where their innate skills might *match* those of men: where judgments were pronounced, where argument and debate were heard, where important transactions were carried out, where policy was determined, and where decisions that profoundly influenced the courses of whole societies were made. Council chambers, courtrooms, public forums—women played no visible part in these settings.

Proper and Improper Heroism

These sexually biased protocols greatly limited and rigidified the definition of heroism. Ambition, enterprise, curiosity, and a whole host of other qualities native to lively minded individuals of either sex were respected in men but were regarded as dangerous and undesirable in women. Assertiveness in women, who were necessary to bear and nurture generations of hunters and warriors and tend to their wounds, seemed a troublesome trait. Gentleness, caution, and consideration of others were considered weaknesses in men but desirable characteristics in women. The Greek myths that celebrated venturesome heroes were matched by many stories that either praised exemplary, docile women like Penelope, who waited patiently (and faithfully) for her husband, Odysseus, to return from the Trojan War, or related cautionary tales about assertive women who came to bad ends, like Cassandra, whose outspoken predictions about the future were disbelieved because of the curse of the god Apollo, whose amorous advances she had rejected.

Women have been heroic in all ages; they would have had to be. This book may serve to remind us of their particular heroism, based on different values and expressed in a different manner. Much of this heroism occurred before silent or unrespected witnesses— other women, young children, prostitutes, invalids—and in circumscribed and humble settings such as orphanages, almshouses, hospitals, prisons. So women's heroism remained anonymous and unpraised and produced no dramatic body of legends or impressive monuments.

For example, in the early 1800s, Elizabeth Fry, a Quaker minister and wife of a wealthy banker, was appalled at the conditions of the women prisoners in Newgate Prison. She recruited other privileged women to join her in setting up a school for younger prisoners and the children who were imprisoned with their mothers. Here the students learned to sew and knit. Fry sought donations of raw materials for the women to make into clothes that they could then sell in a prison shop. In addition the volunteers supplied soap, rags, and clean water for a weekly cleaning day. But the women Fry helped would hardly serve as respected sources in praising her heroism (Anderson and Zinsser, 1988b).

Other women, not so well-off, led lives of unending drudgery, working at home doing piecework or taking in boarders to supplement their husbands' slim wages. Child care was either hard to arrange or inadequate. One man wrote of his memory of his mother, who "came rushing home from Benson's [cotton mill] in the breakfast half hour to give us our breakfast" (Anderson and Zinsser, 1988b, p. 269). This experience must seem familiar to the thousands of working mothers today who do much the same thing, rushing from job to home and family.

Even when women are central figures in history or myth, they themselves do not play heroic roles. Sometimes they appear as *reasons* behind male heroic adventures that actually have different purposes. The male heroes of the Trojan War, for example, might well have used the rescue of the beauteous Helen as a convenient fiction to justify the nationalistic aims of their ambitious kings. In "rescuing" Helen, the Greeks were actually challenging the stranglehold that Troy held over the waterways that the Greek rulers wanted to navigate. Centuries later, in the Victorian period, Britain's Queen Victoria, herself a model of wifely and domestic womanhood, was used as a figurehead to justify the nationalistic ambitions of her male ministers.

Men were supposed to think and be brave; women were to be compliant and pretty. This insipid and lethargic female image is at first glance very different from the "woman of valor" in the Old

Testament who was admired for being active and energetic. But she was a domestic executive who saw to the welfare of her household, gave to the poor, planted vineyards, spun, sewed, and was a model of industry. Even so, the main reason for all this bustle was her family. The Bible records that her *husband* can "safely trust" her and her *children* "call her blessed." When the preservation of an absent husband's estate fell to his wife, she could behave heroically; but then she was seen as rightfully—and merely—serving her husband's welfare.

Our present knowledge shows that even the innate tendencies that differentiate women from men are apparently still very susceptible to environmental pressures. For example, research has observed that newborn boy babies interact more energetically and directly with their environment than do baby girls. Boys are more likely to manipulate objects and move against obstacles. (I return to this topic in Chapter Four.) In ancient societies based on the direct use of force, such traits can be seen as invaluable resources in conquering physical peril and furthering expansionistic aims. These behaviors would have been considered essential characteristics of the hero. We know now what was evidently not known over the centuries: the relationship between heredity and environment is a fluid one, and the roles of women and men are susceptible to environmental dicta. No perfect correlations between sex, behavior, and environmental influence have been established.

Outdated Definitions of Heroism

As dear as the old hero tales may be, the simplistic biases of the myths and fairy tales of humanity's childhood just do not serve the complex needs of a technically skillful and mutually interdependent world. The nature of the civilized world has changed drastically since these legends were first told, and these stories no longer faithfully illuminate our current lives and struggles. Certainly some contemporary personal struggles repeat classic themes. Humankind has always needed, for example, to gather as much information about the universe as possible. But the modern world has developed some radically different patterns and agencies for information gathering and disseminating. The acquisition of information, which was previously based on the tales of a heroic foray into an unfamiliar country, has evolved into on-the-spot coverage of remote exploits. This closeness has permanently altered our image of heroic faces and our traditions of heroic activities. Just contrast what ordinary people knew at those times about the voyages of Marco Polo or the polar explorations of Amundsen and Peary with what the average television viewer knows about our astronauts, some of whom are women.

This means that there are new prospects, undreamed of before, for the inclusion of women in our catalogue of venturesome heroes. Furthermore, the technology of our age has also proved to be an unexpected ally against the old order of things by delivering an unprejudiced supply of energy, one which no longer depends so much on sheer physical strength. Ranging from the riveting machine and the bulldozer to the computer and the fax machine, technology has provided new gender-neutral opportunities previously unavailable. Technological advances have substituted obedient mechanical and electrical power for brute strength.

The combination of our new technology with our lopsided image of heroism could actually set the stage for disaster. The worship of impetuous action, so diverting in our romantic heroes like Clint Eastwood, Rocky, and Batman, could become lethal when we have the means to blast the whole world into oblivion. Technology has invented tools and machinery that amplify the classic heroic traits of strength, speed, and aggression, which makes these characteristics more powerful and much more dangerous. We could argue that women's exclusion from the arts of war has given them a healthful distance from the time-honored ways of dealing with dissension. Now that war is becoming a prohibitively costly way to resolve conflict, women's interpersonal priorities and experiences have become too valuable to overlook.

Our modern mythologists, the media, still perpetuate the standard heroic stereotypes. The range and breadth of behaviors that might successfully counteract stereotyped and sexually biased notions of heroism have yet to be considered dramatic enough to be commercially profitable. The media favor slick and quick presentations of heroic deeds. Television and movies, newspapers and magazines bypass the heroism of women by continuing their habitual skew toward the flamboyant and sensational.

Women who argue against these slanted portrayals are beginning to back up their protests by writing letters to sponsors and by boycotting sponsors' products. Nevertheless, spectacle reigns. The Terminator, Rambo, and other cliché styles of heroism are still favored, copied, and circulated. These images trade on our instinctual and historic appetite for vital heroes; but they are fundamentally escapist and insubstantial, having little relevance to the actual circumstances and experience of the viewer's life. All that the modern viewer can glean from these roles is empty bravado and a vicarious and infantile allegiance to standards from another age. These characters only underscore the emptiness of our current heroic images.

The symbolic importance of having the biggest or the fastest car on the block can make an instant hero in our superhighway age. The heroic image seems as easy to acquire as purchasing a shirt. In its most tragic form, teenagers have killed fellow students just to get the right pair of athletic shoes. The present pantheon of heroes has become a popular caricature of heroism that glorifies acquisitive struggle, glib portraits of "enemies" and "turf," and the quick resort to force.

But there is progress, partly due to the fact that women are less and less willing to settle for obscure satellite or accessory roles. Women are discontent with stories that picture them merely as injured or helpless victim, convenient helper, or seductive reward for the male hero.

Women have long been aware of their own capacities for independent and heroic achievement, and they have begun to call for the freedom to take active roles on a broader stage. They rebel against a subordination that for so long directed their energies to the service of other people's goals. Anonymous heroines of the hearth have energized actions against slavery, poverty, and disenfranchisement. Women's cries for bread started a revolution in France. Women who worked as abolitionists moved on to demand universal suffrage after the Civil War. Women who were boarded together as they worked in the textile mills of New England formed one of the earliest labor unions.

Women want social acknowledgment of the unrecognized heroism they have played out for generations both inside and outside of homey and intimate settings. They also urgently want access to heroic decisions that have customarily been reserved for men.

Heroes: The New Story

In most cultures, the familiar macho pattern of heroism still exists: differences are reduced to single-minded adversarial struggles in which somebody "wins."

The heroes of the modern world must transcend this simplistic posture; the classic hero is unfit to deal with complex interactions in a world of overlapping interests where it is increasingly difficult to identify a clear-cut antagonist. Two valid truths can be learned from mythology and history: the intimidated only wait for their chance to turn the tables, and solutions arrived at by force rather than conviction are unstable and costly.

An emphasis on direct physical action usually means that the courage of articulate but nonviolent objectors is ignored. It becomes easy to overlook the poet who describes the deadly life under an oppressive regime, the publisher of an outlawed paper that prints opposing political positions, the conservationist in a totalitarian regime whose environmental protests arouse the general spirit of protest in his compatriots, or the women who silently parade beneath a dictator's windows with pictures of their "vanished" dissident children.

Female heroism is rooted in the particular circumstances and values of women's lives, where connection and relationship may not be quickly stated in adversarial terms (Gilligan, 1982; Gilligan, Lyons, and Hanmer, 1990; Tannen, 1990). It should come as no surprise, then, that women have been in the forefront of reform movements protesting burdensome taxation on such necessities as bread and salt and have worked to form labor unions, improve working conditions, eliminate sweatshops, and humanize treatment in prisons, workhouses, and hospitals (I will return to this topic later). The concerns of home and family, while certainly not the exclusive domain of women, have primarily been theirs over the centuries. These responsibilities, coupled with women's affiliative skills, have resulted in women becoming a powerful voice for legislative reform, calling for more government involvement and support of child care, education, and public health, opposing drunk driving, and championing positions that advance basic human progress in many forms.

Women's heroism has been equally brave and equally original as that of men. But because in some of its forms it differs from the traditional pattern of heroism, it has often gone unrecognized, even though it may actually contain promising ways for dealing with disagreement and grievance. For example, the very anonymity of women's heroism holds the seeds of progress. A lowered concern for individual prominence (hard to accomplish in the media's search for the latest news) may help create an emphasis on deliberation and reflection. Away from the hubbub of premature publicity, away from the search for winners and losers, conciliatory proposals might get the thoughtful attention they merit. I referred earlier to the miraculous efficiency of our information-processing apparatus; nowhere is it so counterproductive as in the media's interest in reporting the results of summit meetings with almost a scorekeeper's insistence on tangible results.

Women today face some old familiar problems that reflect their historical roles as homemakers and caregivers. But since they have moved outside their traditional roles into territory that was mostly male, they now face unprecedented dilemmas. The standard male solutions do not apply neatly for women, even though women may be in the "same" situations. The recent sensitivity to sexual harassment, for example, is a consequence of the increasing presence of both sexes in what may previously have been the stronghold of only one. What women may say or do with other women—and the way men behave with other men—change when both are working in the same setting. A woman in the office, at a board meeting, or at the controls of an airplane may confront a different set of complications and, even more importantly, may have a different set of values, skills, or channels for coping with her problems than her male colleague. When women express legitimate complaints, for example, they may run up against the male ethos that advises to grin and bear it.

The Heroic Balance

Women's heroic choice differs from that of the classic male hero, who has throughout legend physically *separated* himself from home and family in order to follow his heroic path. The woman hero must also address herself to the world in which she lives, but she does it differently: she emerges from her early close relationship with the smaller intimate setting, but she does not separate herself. The problem she must resolve is how to distinguish herself as an individual *within* familiar environmental pressures. Woman's quest is to balance her independence with her sensitivity to relationship and connection. When she has achieved this equilibrium, when she perceives what she can accomplish through her own independent action, she is free to move from her personal center and relate to her world with a firm sense of agency, independence, and choice. Women have already accomplished much of this, but much more remains to be done.

The woman hero must continue to address and influence the grander society. She must continue to encompass the heroism in her own life and to point to it in the lives of women she knows, and she must encourage it in the lives of all women.

Conclusion

Human welfare still rests on some of the basic survival skills attached to the noble behavior of heroes and on the specific talents that individuals, women as well as men, bring in response to challenge. But our image of heroism is anachronistic and incomplete. It is time to recover the unrecognized half of the heroic story, to look toward a heroism for our times that acknowledges—and puts to good use—the forbidden heroism of women.

TWO

A Population of Heroes

We look out to see what's going on, but then we want to crawl back in; we are afraid to come out. But we shouldn't be. Because the world was made for the women as well as the men. We have a place here too.
　　　　　—Fran L. Buss, *Dignity: Lower Income Women Tell of Their Lives and Struggles*

When we move beyond the classic stereotype, we can see that many ordinary women and men are actually heroes. Furthermore, heroes are more numerous than we may have thought. Although heroes of the everyday may not receive the great acclaim accorded the classic hero, the value of private heroism may be greater precisely because we see everyday heroes up close; they are so near, so intimately connected. They are family, co-workers, neighbors, and their heroism takes place in commonplace settings and in response to everyday challenges.

This very *ordinariness* is particularly relevant to those professionals who deal with human growth and aspiration. Individuals come to therapy in order to transcend a personal crisis, to move from an immobilized posture to a sense of individual possibility. People who enter therapy are looking for release from familiar patterns of interaction that no longer work. To make such changes in one's life is a heroic task that calls for a range of heroic possibilities.

Darlene, the woman quoted in the epigraph at the beginning of this chapter, made her own heroic choice, as did the other lower-income women whose experiences were reported by Buss (1985). Darlene had to resolve a struggle frequently encountered in therapy: the discrepancy between a belittled and impotent image of herself and an intuitive sense of her greater possibilities. At first, Darlene compared herself and other women to mice: scurrying around, taking up little room, living in corners and crevices, making do with scraps and crumbs. Yet she insisted, "We have a place here, too"— her statement of heroic eligibility. So, she got her general equivalency diploma and, confronting her husband's disapproval, went on to take bookkeeping classes. Darlene's sense of entitlement to her "place" testifies to her belief that her life could be more than a parenthetical phrase tucked into the major events that men live. Like all women, she needed a heartening image that could make the crucial difference between resignation and vitality, that could enable her first to envision and then to effect changes.

All ten women in Buss's study told stories of obscure lives crammed with people and events that would have swamped lesser souls. In the face of oppressive odds, despite all their efforts, the best that many of these women could achieve was a precarious balance between independence and despair. Buss describes the struggle of each woman as she confronted obstacles with persistence and courage. Central to these struggles was the search for a personal sense of direction and significance that would give each woman a unique life of dignity and purpose.

Our images of heroes provide an inventory, if you will, of heroic characteristics. And while some of these characteristics may be basic to all heroism, others may be distinctly related to whether the hero is a woman or a man. A useful definition of heroism must include both types.

Five Shared Characteristics of Heroism

Heroism takes many forms. Out of the roster of qualities ascribed to heroes over the ages, I would like to focus on five.

1. All heroes are motivated by a profound respect for human life.
2. Heroes have a strong sense of personal choice and effectiveness.
3. Their perspective on the world is original, going beyond what other people think is possible.
4. They are individuals of great physical and mental courage.
5. Heroes are not measured by publicity. Whether a heroic act

receives worldwide attention or occurs in an obscure setting with only a single witness, a heroic act is still heroic.

Respect for Human Life

The hero profoundly believes in the value and dignity of human life. The one act that most people would agree is heroic is risking one's life to save another. The annual Carnegie Hero Fund Commission endorses this opinion by giving medals and cash awards to women or men who have saved lives. In 1990, eight women won awards for acts ranging from saving people from assault to rescuing people from runaway automobiles or from drowning (Carnegie Hero Fund Commission, 1990). Mythology is full of hero tales about unfortunate victims apparently doomed if not for the intervention of the hero.

But respect for human life may take other forms, Antigone, the daughter of Oedipus, the incestuous King of Thebes, is a passionate example from Greek literature. After Oedipus's self-imposed exile, he left his two sons, Eteocles and Polynices, to alternate in ruling the kingdom. Eteocles ruled first and refused to give up the throne when it was his brother's turn. His refusal led to a fratricidal battle in which both brothers were killed. Creon, their uncle, ascended the throne and decreed that Eteocles should be buried with full honors. Polynices was to be left to rot on the battlefield, and anyone who attempted to bury him would be executed. Antigone argued that Polynices be treated with dignity, even in death, and went out herself to bury him. Creon, with ironic cruelty, ordered her buried alive.

Valuing life can also mean preserving the dignity with which a life is to be lived. I remember how Shirley, a social worker, described her pain and fear when she risked her own safety in confrontations with abusive and antagonistic parents who believed she had no right to interfere in "family affairs." Shirley's devotion to children's welfare is fed by her faith that she can do something to ensure that the children's future can be different from the ugliness that surrounds them. She has to work hard for the private victories that she pulls off. For example, she told me about her joy at helping a bright youngster be admitted to a special summer program in spite of her mother's apathy about filling out the proper application forms and her subtle sabotage about getting her daughter to the special bus on time. The mother "forgot" the time of departure, even though Shirley had called to remind her. Then there was something wrong with the car. At the last minute, Shirley arranged for someone to pick the daughter up.

Marian volunteers in a shelter for battered wives. She often serves as an intermediary between the woman and her angry, brutal husband. Marian tells what she has learned about intimidation from her firsthand experience with angry husbands who come storming in to reclaim their wives. She preaches insurrection when she tells the women that victimization is not inevitable. At the same time, she also seeks to understand what makes the man behave so brutally. She wants *neither* the husband nor the wife to be doomed to their present roles.

Women have historically been in the forefront of the insistence on humane principles and treatment when these have been denied to undervalued or silent victims of an indifferent society. The women who fought to remove the term *illegitimate* from birth certificates were doing this. The women who currently protest against the degraded portrayals of women in advertising and in pornography are fighting for their dignity. So, too, are the advocates of comparable wages, safe working conditions, and adequate medical care.

Many of the chores that women have quietly but heroically performed over the years have been the simple services that support the dignity and welfare of the people in their care, adults as well as children. Feeding, clothing, and keeping others clean are all humble tasks, but how quickly a life deteriorates when these basic needs go untended. Many women have faced overwhelming odds— and many continue to face them—on untamed and unpublicized frontiers: in the schools and clinics of our city slums, in wartime hospitals, collecting and distributing food and clothing to the homeless. All ways of preserving lives.

Faith in Her Effective Exercise of Choice

The hero has a profound faith in herself as an essential influential force. An unhappy circumstance is not simply to be endured. Personal action is called for, and she *chooses* to act. She balances her own energy against the opposition and moves to make changes. Mary Robinson, for example, worked to unionize the J. P. Stevens textile mill, passing out leaflets (when she knew she might be arrested for doing that in a "company town"), speaking up at stockholder's meetings, and questioning the president of the company about the health and safety measures taken at the plant to prevent brown lung disease, lost limbs, varicose veins, and hearing loss (Buss, 1985).

Another heroic woman who went beyond resignation is Betty Washington. She set herself and others to work toward their common goal. She singlehandedly recruited and organized people for a citizen's watch program to rid her Boston neighborhood of the drug dealing and crime that were threatening to take it over. This made her a publicly marked target, vulnerable to reprisal. But here is how a modern hero talks: "Either you speak out and take the risk, or you die in the cesspool" ("Heroes, Past and Present," 1987, p. 63).

Sometimes the hero's insistence on choice and impact is directed toward an existing institution that has become dysfunctional. One woman, disgusted with the sloppy and dangerous conditions in the public housing project in St. Louis where she lived, formed a tenants' organization to monitor the safety and maintenance of the project. She interviewed prospective tenants and formed a tenants' committee to set up rules about keeping the hallways and public areas swept. In another struggle, some mothers protesting the dangerous conditions in the corridors of a local school were not content to wait for the school authorities to respond to their concern about the safety of their children. Instead, the women organized a group of parent-monitors who personally policed the halls.

The heroic woman believes, and reminds others, that common experience and accepted opinion can be changed, and she is willing to be the catalyst, even though she may confront opposition and criticism. Women who petition to be admitted to the priesthood, ministry, or rabbinate of their respective religions are no longer willing to settle for subordinate and indirect access to their God. They advocate that those who perform God's ceremonies on earth must be both female and male. But this petition has serious implications, not the least of which is its challenge to the nature of human communication with God. Women seek to revise "what religious rhetoric assumes: that the men form the legitimate body of the community, while women are allowed to participate only when they assimilate themselves to men" (Pagels, 1979, p. 49).

When I first met Ingrid, she felt dissatisfied with her comfortable life. Her children were grown and gone, and she had time and energy to spare. But her vigor was festering into self-criticism and depression. What could she do with her good energy and free time? She came up with an idea: starting with the markets and restaurants she patronized, Ingrid set up a regular route of restaurants and food stores, picking up food that they had to discard and distributing it to shelters for the homeless.

Grace, a former patient of mine who is a minister, had a vision of her church as an agent for change. She has organized groups that meet, either regularly or on a onetime basis, to discuss problems related to married couples, teenagers, childrearing, interracial relationships, and caring for elderly parents. These groups ranged well beyond the Bible study, bake sale, and prayer groups that usually occupied the church calendar. The reaction from some members of the congregation was not favorable; many of them felt Grace had gone beyond the original path for the church. Indeed she has, but she also increased the participation of some younger people who felt that the church had not been dealing with problems of their generation. In therapy she dealt with her ambivalence. Grace was troubled by the complaints of the more traditional congregants who feel she has gone too far; she doesn't want to lose them either. But she is unwilling to abandon the vision she has for her ministry. She has made some progress by polling the congregation at large and asking them to suggest topics. One of the new groups to be formed deals with the concerns of older congregants, the very ones she was afraid of losing.

Original Perspective

The hero has an original perspective that distinguishes her from others who settle for agreement and conformity or are too beaten down to ask necessary questions. The relationship between the hero and the established order of things is fluid; she insists on her freedom to perceive, within the context of things-as-they-are, the way things *could* be. She moves beyond Eve's example by welcoming her inquisitive turn of mind. Like Eve, she doesn't accept unexplained and timeworn observations; unlike Eve, she has no doubts about her entitlement to information. Her energy gobbles up knowledge for its own sake, and she is unwilling to settle for previous stale levels of knowledge or understanding.

Doubting the inevitable rightness of unquestioned assumptions has gotten women into trouble ever since Eve. It leads to unwelcome questions, but it opens a new view of old behavior. Looking at voting privileges in an untraditional light, the suffragists began to question the historic restriction of the vote to white male property owners only. The trite answer—that there was a classic precedent, that this policy had been good enough for ancient Athenians—did not satisfy. In our own times, the whistle-blower exposes wrongdoing, fraud, or inefficiency in her or his workplace, where one is not supposed to rock the boat. Rocking the boat, however leaky it may be, requires an original perspective and involves the risk of reprisal, slander, ridicule, demotion, and even loss of job.

Cora Lee Johnson in Soperton, Georgia, took a new look at a number of projects, all of which involved informing people about their rights to certain benefits, such as medical aid, low-income housing, and food stamps. After attending a series of workshops sponsored by the Rural Black Women's Leadership Project, she recognized the importance of initiative in action: "They taught us our rights, but then when we walked out that door, it was up to us to go back into our communities and use them" ("Heroes for Hard Times," 1988, p. 30).

Courage

It is almost redundant to say that heroism requires courage, both physical and mental; personal cost takes a backseat to getting the job done. The traditional hero often risks death or injury. In our sensationalistic age, the defiance of death has become one of the accepted signs of heroism. In disregarding her personal welfare, the hero may *appear* to be courting death. This is an oversimplification. In truth, she simply considers the risk of death or injury to be less important than her purpose.

Women unconcerned with personal sacrifice have often given years of devoted service to a cause or a person. They have persisted at unconventional efforts with little recognition or encouragement, willingly surrendering their personal comfort in order to pursue their goals. One example is Marie Curie, who persevered in her research in the face of the disrespect and open disapproval of women scientists that characterized her time (and that still taint our own). Mother Theresa, whose lifelong devotion to the victims of poverty and disease is known throughout the world, is another compelling example.

Heroic courage requires more than simple physical strength; stamina, persistence, and focus are needed. The hero can tolerate high levels of stress and not be overwhelmed. Distractions can be ignored; even necessities may be forgotten. Challenge mobilizes the hero; she meets it with concentration and ingenuity. In moments of crisis or opportunity, her perceptual focus is sharpened rather than dulled. Her behavior is on target: specific, efficient, and aware of, but not restricted by, circumstance.

A chilling example of deadly courage, sharply focused and perfectly targeted, is the story of a doomed woman in a Nazi concentration camp. On her way to the gas chamber she was ordered to dance by an SS officer who knew she had been a dancer and evidently could not resist one last cruel gesture. Listen: "As she danced, she approached him, seized his gun, and shot him down" (Des Pres, 1976, p. 161). In the face of death she heroically ordered her priorities and took her death in her own hands, transcending her tragedy.

The mental courage of the hero permits her to be aware of accepted "truths" and yet not be restricted by them. When the child in the fairy tale says loudly that the emperor isn't wearing any clothes, that child speaks from innocence, not from courage. The heroic woman, however, knows the danger and nevertheless asserts an unwelcome truth. But she speaks from the integrity of the clear-sighted. For her, it isn't enough merely to *think* the unorthodox; she chooses to espouse it publicly.

Irene Mack Pyawasit is one woman who took on a public

challenge by speaking out to redress the injustices faced by Native American students. She works to recruit these students for the University of Wisconsin. She worked to block Exxon from setting up a copper mine that could have polluted the rice beds and the water systems of the nearby Indian reservations (Buss, 1985).

Such heroes are willing to be first to venture into intimidating territories and experiences, encouraging others who follow to find ways to apply their examples to their situation. Fritz Redl (1942, p. 573) calls this "the magic of the initiatory act." He suggests that the initiatory act releases those who follow from feelings of guilt and fear. Extrapolating from Redl, we can see that initiatory magic can range all the way from daring physical exploits to espousing controversial positions. The heroic act can release other women from guilt as well as fear, thereby empowering them to oppose unjust or unfair conditions.

Risky business, going first—for several reasons. To begin with, the hero as pathfinder has little information about the dangers or surprises that may await. Bethenia Owens-Adair wanted to go to Jefferson Medical College in Philadelphia in 1878. She did not get in because her admission depended on a board of regents who, in the words of one of the college's leading professors, "would simply be shocked, scandalized and enraged at the mere mention of admitting a woman" (Luchetti, 1982, p. 183). When she insisted that she wanted a *fine* medical education, better than what was available at the Women's Medical School, she was advised to apply to the University of Michigan, which did admit women. She got her degree there two years later and practiced medicine in the Northwest until her retirement in 1905.

Going first, the hero may also arouse envy or resentment in others when she succeeds, derision or blame when she fails. Dr. Owens-Adair described the hostility of the male doctors in her adopted community to the "new 'Philadelphia' doctor." But she met confrontation with excitement and pride; when her male colleagues unexpectedly challenged her to do an autopsy on the genitals of a male cadaver, she did it coolly and competently (Luchetti, 1982).

Since the heroic act may involve going against the habits and customs of the community, opposition is inevitable; supporters of the status quo do not happily welcome disagreement. The hero needs the mental and emotional stamina to sustain energy and intelligence in the face of personal loss, disapproval, or ostracism. Obviously, one of the most powerful sanctions a community can impose is the threat of ostracism or expulsion. This can be formal, as when a society executes, expels, or jails its dissidents, or informal, as in exclusion from social interactions, passing people over for promotions, or ridicule that isolates psychologically.

Public or Unpublic Heroism

Public heroes are what we usually think of when we think of heroes. They have great impact and are noble examples for a number of people. Drama, awe, and admiration accompany them, and recognition is underscored by ceremonies that accord them even more fame.

But the grandness of these celebrations can sometimes overshadow a far more pervasive and important factor in the lives of most people: the heroes of the intimate setting. The actions of parents, teachers, relatives, neighbors, and occasionally even strangers provide an immediacy that profoundly colors a person's life.

Experiences in therapy can uncover such figures. Therapy looks to recover valuable forgotten resources that are still vital sources of personal support and inspiration. One of my patients, for example, lived a horrendous childhood wracked with pain from a sexually and physically abusive father and a mother who simply ignored what she was unwilling to see. As an adult, Burt still suffers from the expectation that the world is a place where harsh treatment is inescapable. Somewhere in the kindly and helpful adult he had become, there still lived the frightened child, huddled in the corner of a dark closet. One morning I asked him if there had been *any* kind characters in his childhood. He leaned back, and his eyes moistened as he spoke softly of one man on his paper route who had made it a point to be on the front porch when Burt went by and always exchanged a greeting and a smile. What a small rebuttal to his family's treatment of him. But the impact on Burt was profound. He was ready to begin talking about the friends in his present life, who also treated him with respect and affection. For a moment, the man on his boyhood paper route *represented* the supportive forces in his life. The neighbor was a hero who gave Burt a sense of worth and respect that countered the insult of his home life.

All heroism is characterized by these five basic traits I have just described: respect for human life, faith in one's ability to make a difference, original perspective, physical and mental courage, and public or unpublic impact. They are not all equally evident in every heroic life or act; sometimes one or another may dominate. These five characteristics do not constitute a hierarchy of heroism; they are not intended to provide a scale on which heroism can be rated. They are guidelines by which we can recognize the heroism that fills our everyday experience. They help us to appreciate heroism in its ordinary guise, unaccompanied by background music or special effects, and to find the heroic elements in our own lives.

Differences in Female and Male Heroism

Although women and men share many heroic traits, there are also important stylistic *differences* in heroic attitude and action. Women sometimes may duplicate male heroics. But these acts of women have all too often been dismissed as atypical; women have displayed "masculine bravery" or a "courage above her sex" (Fraser, 1984, pp. 163–164). The differences between female and male heroism are not based exclusively on physiology or economic circumstance. They reflect both ideas about the "proper behavior" for each sex and the particular talents of each.

The woman hero usually relies less on muscular strength than her male counterpart and invents other ways to achieve a desired end. Women rely more on persuasion and argument. They also attend as much to the manner in which something is done as to the ultimate purpose. The woman hero may find alternatives to direct confrontation, for example, finding common purposes that make opposition unnecessary. Or since simply overpowering an opponent is unlikely, she may just doggedly outlast whatever stands in her way. Nien Cheng, for example, stubbornly refused to "confess" to sins against the Communist regime in China and eventually outlasted her interrogators. Her imprisonment, which achieved nothing for her captors, finally became an embarrassment to them (Cheng, 1986).

"Proper behavior" has always been a rationale for controlling women. Eve is to be subservient to Adam; Pygmalion sculpts Galatea, his own ideal woman; Penelope is the ideal wife, faithful to her husband through a twenty-year absence (with only a touch of deceitfulness that she employs to protect her husband's kingdom). The woman of valor, the Bible tells us, is praised by her husband and children.

Heroic women, however, have always gone beyond the confines of "proper behavior." Indeed, sometimes the very act of challenging these boundaries has been the heroic deed. Queen Esther ventured uninvited into the presence of her royal husband, who could have had her executed for such daring. Deborah was an outspoken judge, who did not hesitate to express her judgments forcefully. And we have already seen the consequences of Antigone's defiance of Creon's edict.

The circumstances that arouse women's heroic response are often intensely personal. Women are mobilized by the plight of people with whom they feel a compassionate connection and are less aroused to support abstract principles. Women who have achieved some prominence in the arts, sciences, and government, for example, have spoken out publicly in support of a pro-choice position on abortion and have disclosed how abortion affected their own lives. Other famous women have come forward to talk about painful histories involving rape, child abuse, or family alcoholism. They do this in hopes of helping other women with similar experiences. Such public disclosure is heroic—and costly in loss of public approval and support.

Connection

Not only is women's heroism more likely than men's to be a response to events in women's personal spheres, but it is inspired by a sense of women's *connection* to other people with whom they feel a strong bond of kinship. This kinship may be based on family ties, or it may reflect a connection with people perceived to be in the same plight. Much of women's heroism is pervaded by a strong sense of the other, who is also like.

Harriet Tubman is an excellent representative of the magnetism of kinship. She has been called the Moses of her people for bringing them out of slavery. She had escaped, and she could have lived on with her individual victory. But she went back again and again in disguise to Southern plantations to lead caravans of escaped slaves north to freedom. Similarly, Jane Pittman asserted not only her own equality but also the equality of her black sisters and brothers when she dared to drink from a "whites only" fountain. Corazon Aquino moved into the forefront of political action to continue the struggle begun by her assassinated husband against a corrupt regime in the Philippines. Winnie Mandela confronted the oppressive government in South Africa that imprisoned her husband, Nelson, for almost thirty years. Countless dedicated teachers have risen above discouraging school experiences and gone back to pull younger versions of themselves out of similar despair.

Frequently women's heroism centers around the identification of danger or injustice at a grassroots level, in circumstances that involve them or their neighbors or loved ones personally (Randall, 1982). So it is not surprising that so many protests against environmental pollution begin with women's awareness of higher-than-normal incidences of disease in their children and their neighbors. It seems a simple extension of personal concern and affiliation.

Joyce Maynard (1987, p. D6) writes about Jean Gump, a sixty-year-old mother of twelve who is serving eight years (eight years!) in a federal penitentiary for "non-violent acts of protest at a nuclear-weapons site." Maynard calls Gump "the woman who taught me that part of looking after our children means looking after our world, too."

Fairness or Responsibility

Carol Gilligan, in her classic study of the moral values of women and men, enriches our distinction between heroism in the service of connection and heroism in the service of an abstract principle. She observes that moral judgments of men are likely to be made on the

basis of "fairness," while the judgments of women more likely rest
on the basis of personal "care and responsibility" (1982, p. 73).

No sensible argument would try to establish which of these
two values, fairness or responsibility, is superior. It is important,
though, to look at some of the implications of Gilligan's distinction
because moral judgments strongly influence the heroic response.

Fairness. This is an abstraction often defined by arbitrary
criteria. Fairness implies a set of rules or a code governing behaviors
that are justified and tolerable under certain circumstances. Fairness
is frequently a judgment made about the outcome of a specific
event, with the full awareness that the decision may well become a
precedent in subsequent events. The game stops, for example, until
the correct application of the rules is determined; personal need or
preference has little to do with the decision. Whatever feelings may
emerge must be dealt with privately as they are not considered a part
of the process.

Fairness invokes a rational and orderly world (which is also,
alas, an abstraction). It is a theoretical ethic that governs the deal-
ings among *people who qualify* and whose position in a hierarchical order depends on mutual agreement about rules. But
qualification has all too often been implicitly based on an exclu-
sionary system of eligibility. Anyone who does not measure up to
the specific standards of the members is not included within the
system's arrangements; although subject to the system's rules, they
are powerless in formulating them. Underneath the rubric of "fairness" we can discern an arbitrary assumption of equality based on
disqualifying those who are not similar to the founding members
of the society.

The framers of the U.S. Constitution, for example, felt that
they had ensured representative and evenhanded voting rights under
the law. But they were propertied white males who, in a spirit of
fairness, granted those rights to other propertied white males. This
skewed sense of fairness also appears in war. Combatants identify
their enemy as subhuman in order to deal with him in a way they
would not treat comrades. "All's fair in love and war" is not really
a relaxation of the rules; it is actually a repeal. Fairness, it seems,
can have a hidden off/on switch.

Responsibility. On the other hand, responsibility is a rheostatic response that recognizes a continuum of experience. It does not calculate equality but reasons instead on a scale of relationship. continuity, and environmental complexity. Responsibility brings shades of grey into absolute values like fairness, precedent, and consistency by adding considerations such as consequence and reaction. The definition of responsibility implies an act carried out "in response to."

These responses, however, are not made to sets of rules but to specific situations and people whose personal needs and preferences must be considered regardless of their parity in terms of power or resources. The dominant elements here are personal; they are expressed in flexible human values rather than set statistical values dealing in precedents and percentages.

From their beginnings with the personal, women often move on to more global issues. The mothers and wives of the victims of oppression in South America, for example, illuminated abstract principles of democratic license through the experiences of individual torment. These women maintained their persistent vigil under the windows of the dictators, carrying photographs of their husbands and children who had disappeared. Unable to overcome by strength of arms, they prevail through quiet, indomitable confrontation. Although this did not bring back their dead, it spoke to their countrymen and to the world.

Let us not make the mistake of assuming that an interest in relationship and responsibility leaves women uninterested in fairness. Women do take heroic stances in the name of fairness, but the sense of fairness is rooted in relationship and responsibility. Beulah Mae Donald, a black woman whose son had been lynched, confronted and sued the Ku Klux Klan in Alabama. She was interested in fairness, even though she knew that the unfairness that had taken her son was irreversible. There was still a measure of fairness to be had. What she wanted was to clear her murdered son's name, to let everyone know what had happened and that he had done no wrong (Kornbluth, 1987).

A patient of mine, whom I will call Zenia, exhibited similar courage. She was incensed by the unfairness of the discipline protocol at her son's school. Although she was frightened at taking a

stand, Zenia went to the principal of the school with recommenda-
tions about setting up a board made up of teachers, parents, and
student representatives to handle conflicts. To do this she had to
confront and move past her own childhood experience in a very
strict religious school where questioning authority was unheard of.
The exhilaration Zenia felt when her proposal was endorsed by
other parents as well as school staff was deeply satisfying.

The women today who speak against war and nuclear escalation are not basing their arguments on what's fair, tallying the
number of weapons each side has and deciding that one missile
system is equal to three radar-equipped planes or some such impossible arithmetic. They reckon the cost in human lives and in a bleak
wintry future for the whole world. These women see themselves as
agents for change, and they are willing to put their personal welfare
at the service of this pursuit. They have taken the initiatory step.
By doing so, they have made it possible for others to add their
voices.

Aggregate or Solo Action

Another distinctive quality of women's heroism is that it often takes
the form of aggregate action. Women band together to achieve a
level of power they could not reach singly. Grim stories of Nazi
concentration camps contrast men and women: "men, who tended
to be 'lone wolves,' [while] women formed surrogate families, becoming each other's 'sisters,' 'daughters,' or 'mothers' as their real
families perished. . . . Almost all female survivors testify that they
would not have lived without the help and support of other
women" (Anderson and Zinsser, 1988b, p. 319).

Women's political action has too often been a subsidiary
effort, self-effacing and indirect. Until recently, women have overwhelmingly been supporters of candidates rather than candidates
themselves. Nevertheless, in the service of their candidates and
causes, women have gone heroically into hostile territory with petitions and speeches, risking disapproval and derision, organizing
small cadres of like-minded people to speak out and unite in confronting a common adversary.

Working in the aggregate has its drawbacks as far as the

heroism of women is concerned. It virtually guarantees the anonymity of women heroes, each of whom may have performed an individual act of great courage but who has submerged her own identity in the service of a common cause. The loss for women is that there are too few individual names to recite. We have only a meager roster of publicly acknowledged female heroes to hearten individual women in their solitary dilemmas.

But there are some women we should know by name. The Grimke sisters, Angelina and Sarah, are examples of female heroism from pre–Civil War times. They were so passionately devoted to the abolitionist cause that they left their home in the South and worked for years in the Philadelphia Female Antislavery Society. They found a publisher for Sarah Douglass's account of her life as a black schoolteacher. They tirelessly recruited hundreds of new members for female antislavery societies in Massachusetts, and they obtained thousands of signatures on antislavery petitions that they then forwarded to their representatives in Congress (Lerner, 1979).

Sarah Grimke, like many other women of the abolitionist movement, also worked for equal rights for women. Protesting the age-old link between assertive women and Eve, she wrote:

> Woman, I am aware, stands charged to the present day with having brought sin into the world. I shall not repel the charges by any counter assertions, although as was hinted, Adam's ready acquiescence with his wife's proposal does not savor much of that superiority in strength of mind that is arrogated by man. Even admitting that Eve was the greater sinner, it seems to me that man might be satisfied with the dominion he has claimed and exercised for nearly six thousand years. . . . I ask no favors for my sex. I surrender not our claim to equality. All I ask of our brethren is that they will take their feet from off our necks [Stone, 1976, p. 231].

The formation of labor unions in the early 1900s—under male leadership, although a great many factory workers were female—was stormy and uncertain. An early strike against one shirtwaist company (an industry that employed mostly women) appeared to be coming to an ineffectual end. At a meeting of the workers, there was a parade of several of the male labor union leaders urging action, but the meeting was dragging on to no apparent resolution until a frail teenage girl named Clara Lemlich rose to say passionately: "I am a working girl, one of those striking against intolerable conditions. I am tired of listening to speakers who talk in generalities. What we are here for is to decide whether or not to strike. I offer a resolution that a general strike be declared—now" (Howe, 1976, p. 298).

Her words were very simple, and they electrified the meeting. A general strike was called immediately. Although the picketing was carried out by the young immigrant women (mostly Italian and Jewish) who actually worked in the factories, many middle-class American women rallied to their support. Again, connection, relationship.

Exploration or Civilization

Still another difference between the heroism of women and men lies in the male tradition of exploration of new territory and the accompanying vision of profitable expansion. The physical act of exploration has long been a male privilege. McGrath (1985, p. 14) speculates that for American men "the frontier experience was the source of the most important myth—the belief that men could regenerate themselves by conquering 'virgin' lands."

Expeditions of conquest and exploration were usually funded either through royal patronage or by commercial interests in the hope that the discovery would repay the sovereign or business sponsor with riches, political dominance, or power. Historically, few women have had royal power or wealth in the first place, and even fewer women had enough influence in business to request or obtain backing. More recently, for every aviatrix like Amelia Earhart or Beryl Markham there are a dozen Lindberghs, Amundsens, and Pearys. For every astronaut like Sally Ride there are twenty Neil Armstrongs. True to precedent, our nationally sponsored exploration of outer space explicitly carries with it the ambition of colonizing and industrializing our universe. Until recently all our astronauts were men. The sponsors are modern equivalents of royalty: big business and government.

In contrast with heroic male explorers, countless anonymous women heroes seem less interested in "regenerating" themselves. The male wave of exploration is almost always followed by an invasion of women who tame what has already been discovered. Women move into the harsh territory and work the land, make homes and raise families there, and then go about establishing the schools, hospitals, and other institutions that community life calls for. This isn't considered heroic, although it often calls for hours of relentless labor and persistence in the face of discouraging odds. It's "women's work"—not the stuff of which traditional heroism is made.

Sara Evans (1989) has observed that these voluntary communal activities helped women carve out a new area of influence, the "public" stage of institutions designed to serve community needs. Actually this moved women beyond their purely "private" home-bound activities because it extended their caretaking skills to public welfare.

Force or Persuasion

One further difference between male and female heroism is men's greater reliance on bodily strength, obviously a capacity more limited in women. Men hone themselves by confronting physical challenges in racing, hunting, mountain climbing, and other recreational activities. Additionally, school athletic budgets are weighted overwhelmingly in favor of support for those sports played by men.

Men's physical prowess and cultural training may predispose them to use force in those instances where they cannot easily persuade. Furthermore, they are celebrated for doing so.

The use of persuasion rather than force is a particularly feminine form of heroism. Like much female behavior it has not been recognized as the stuff of which heroism is made. Early verbal proficiency (as we shall see in Chapter Four), as well as inferior strength, may have inclined women to find ways of influencing their adversaries without having to overpower them.

Women also know the power of the written word. Harriet

Beecher Stowe, who wrote *Uncle Tom's Cabin,* is a celebrated example. Abraham Lincoln recognized her as the little lady who started the war. And there are others.

Carolina Maria de Jesus wrote about her life in a Brazilian slum. A reporter once heard her berating a group of men who were beating some children, threatening to put them in her "book" (her diary of life in a slum of São Paulo). The reporter asked if he could run excerpts of her diary in his newspaper. The excerpts created a sensation. They were finally published in a book, which has outsold every book printed in Brazil. Carolina writes: "The politicians knew that I am a poetess. And that a poet will even face death when he sees his people oppressed" (Moffat and Painter, 1975, p. 294).

Fanny Kemble, a famous actress in the early 1800s, was married for a while to a wealthy slave owner. The ownership of slaves horrified her. She wrote *Journal of a Residence on a Georgia Plantation in 1838–39,* which poignantly described the inhumanity of slavery as she had witnessed it. The manuscript was published during the Civil War, and her husband was outraged. He divorced her, took custody of their children, and left her with no income. She returned to the stage with great success (Moffat and Painter, 1975), but at what personal cost!

If women are so effective at using words, why are they so underrepresented in the fields of diplomacy and arbitration? For one thing, they still have to deal with the stereotype that women should limit themselves to home and family and not engage in public, global matters. Diplomatic arenas have been closed to women since the beginning of recorded time.

In industrialized countries, women are now being trained as arbitrators and organizational consultants. Their skill at negotiating compromise and teaching better communication is being recognized throughout industry and government agencies.

I have known a number of women in therapy who are highly successful in these specialties. Eleanor, for example, works very effectively in organizational arbitration within public service agencies. One day she commented to me that her first task is to make sure she has the respect of the policemen and firemen with whom she works. Of course this is true for all outside "experts" called into an organization; but for her as a woman, Eleanor was aware that this task carried an extra psychological charge.

In a workshop in a large European city, Phyllis described one week's work teaching the police department how to interact with the people they meet in the line of duty. In her account, the first task was to examine the ways the police had of not listening to *her*. Their discounting of what she had to offer came from a sense that a woman could not have much to teach them. Through examining this attitude the police came to see how they acted the same way toward other "civilians" as well.

Conclusion

Once we move beyond archaic stereotypes of heroism, it is apparent that heroes are both more numerous and more diverse than we thought. Such an abundance of heroes, fully perceived and valued, offers a wide range of heroic options, a heartening diversity. This does not *diminish* the power of the traditional heroic image to encourage and inspire; it *enlarges* it. The expanded sense of heroic possibility can make the difference between an individual feeling like an isolated victim of immutable influences or like a person who might directly take a more central role in shaping the events of her own life.

Although women's heroism shares some common aspects with male heroism, it also reflects its own social and psychological options and talents. Heroism occurs in modest, undramatic settings as well as in sensational scenes of tension and danger. When we move beyond simplistic definition, heroism is equally within the capacities of both women and men.

THREE

Entitled to Be a Hero

Myths are the sanctuaries of language where our meanings
for "male" and "female" are stored.
　　　　　—Alicia S. Ostriker, *Stealing the Language*

Calling a woman who has done something heroic a *hero* is much
more than simply naming her correctly. It not only acknowledges
that *she* personally has behaved as a hero; it also allows the possibility that the description might apply to *all* women. Even further,
the concept of heroism is enlarged to include some previously overlooked heroic behavior by *men* as well as women.

Children who are beginning to talk learn names first: mama,
water, ball. Referring to something by its proper name is a huge
improvement over just pointing to it. It's a giant leap out of one-
dimensional experience, out of a flat world into a round one that
expands dramatically into dimensions of time, space, and continuity.

The right name confers mastery over time and circumstance.
It makes something—a cookie, a glass of milk—appear when we
want it. Before naming, something existed only so long as it stood
in front of us. When it was gone, it vanished, leaving hardly a trace.
Nouns were childhood's magic incantations, ensuring substance
and longevity. A name could conjure up memory, making the image of the named person or object clearer, more lasting, and personally relevant.

Confidence in the power of naming increased as we grew
older and more verbal. Calling each other by names gave us a sense

of authority and jurisdiction, like small versions of Adam naming the creatures in the Garden of Eden. We named someone; therefore that person was.

The ability to use the right name is also critical for conceptualizing experience. This faculty is often lost to people I have seen in therapy. The cover-ups of their childhood have either given them the wrong words with which to describe their feelings or have deprived them of adequate language. This lack leaves people with a fuzzy sense of their own directions as well as an uneasy sense of never quite being understood.

Winifred, one of my patients, had been reared as an "army brat" whose family norms stressed not asking questions. The implicit standard was like the charge of the Light Brigade: "Theirs not to question why, Theirs but to do or die." But this requirement was stifling her. Since it was wrong to ask questions, she consequently felt ill at ease in a world where everybody else seemed to know what they were doing and what they wanted. For her to be heroic called for a big stretch in her customary limits in expressiveness. This was literally unthinkable for her; it became clear in therapy that she actually couldn't even *think* of questions.

When we began to work together, she was a single mother, very competent at her cut-and-dried statistical job. Since Winifred believed she had to take things as they came, she felt she had no choice of friends or activities and pretty much limited herself to taking care of her young son. One afternoon, in response to my request, she rattled off a recital of the family do's and don'ts as they had been taught to her in her childhood. In order to intensify what she was saying, I asked her to imagine a scene in which she would instruct her son to behave as she had been told. She paused a moment, and this time she rebelled; she said she didn't want to squelch him that way. The word *squelched*, when applied to the bright, energetic little boy she loved, was intolerable. But until she could put the rules into words and then use them against her own child, she wasn't able to question them. We then went on to practice, with her asking me questions about the furnishings of my office. Scared at first (as she put it, how dare she criticize me?), she soon got better, even venturing into criticism—something I hadn't bargained for—which pleased both of us as evidence of her quick progress.

The Lifelong Search for Heroes

Although children continue to look to family members and intimates for example and encouragement, they soon are attracted to
stories, including fairy tales. The teller of fairy tales wants to en-
chant the listener and sketch a drama where behaviors are either
rewarded or punished. In the evenhanded treatments of fairy tales,
boy or girl heroes live side by side in the enchanted realms. One can
choose between Jack and the beanstalk or Little Red Riding Hood,
between Ali Baba and his forty thieves or Goldilocks and her three
bears. Later, in the adventurous stories of childhood, the pickings
get slimmer. Even then, there is the choice between the exploits of
a little girl in Wonderland or a cabin boy on Treasure Island.

Every good teller of tales knows that if you are telling a story
to a little girl, you will fare better if you have a little girl as its main
character. Lewis Carroll knew this when he delighted a real little
girl named Alice with his "love gift of a fairy tale." My father knew
this. His bedtime stories always centered around the adventures of
a little girl, just about my age. This little girl, it seems, was always
in the middle of some adventure or another. What was wonderful
about these tales was that although she was a brave and resourceful
character, she would sometimes get into a predicament over her
head. Then, she would call on her Unseen Friend, who would offer
a suggestion or occasionally would intervene, and, hooray, she
would get out of trouble. Paternalistic? Of course it was. I was eight
or nine years old, and the narrator, remember, was my father. But
it also taught me that the *world* was my arena, not the kitchen and
the elementary school. To me, my father was a hero, opening my
mind to what seemed like endless inviting possibilities.

It's clear that fairy tales serve other useful purposes for the
child. Through the adventures of the hero—boy or girl, prince or
princess—the child reflects on the dangers overcome in the tale and
sees how they fit into the circumstances of her own life (Bettelheim,
1977). The heroism of the child, identifying with the fairy tale heroine while remaining safely outside danger, at this point is vicarious. The child even exerts a kind of mastery over distressing events
by knowing (in most cases) the end of the story.

The little girl can generalize from stories where the admirable or canny heroine ultimately triumphs over adversity. The fairy tale reassures her that honesty, persistence, ingenuity, and courage will serve her well. Just like the fairy tale character, she is beginning to explore an environment that presents her with the unexpected and is full of strange contingencies and consequences. When she applies these lessons to her own life, she can feel optimistic and capable. Her identification with the fairy tale heroine serves her developing sense of mastery.

Sometimes, in response to an impasse in therapy, I have asked a patient to name her favorite childhood fairy tale character and then to imagine what this character would tell her about her current dilemmas.

One afternoon, when I asked Adriana which fairy tale character came to mind, she replied, "Snow White." I asked her to speak of her life as if she were Snow White. Adriana described how beautiful her mother was and how, because of her own feelings of inferiority, she had chosen embittered people to be her friends, joining them in their isolation. Due to her mother's own vanity, Adriana came to consider herself not beautiful—in a world where beauty is given high priority. She felt unable to compete and so quit the home scene entirely. The parallel to the Snow White story is close; when Snow White became aware of her stepmother's jealousy, she also left home. Her heroic act was to run away. We talked about the story, and Adriana began to see that leaving home was just the *first* move toward independence. Our work could then shift to helping Adriana develop a sense of what she wanted out of her life and not waste her energy in reaction to her mother's self-preoccupation. Adriana discovered that she wanted to be a potter. She looked around and found an artist who would let her be an apprentice in his studio. The connection *she* wanted with beauty was to create it, not to look for it in the mirror.

The Heroes of Childhood

Adventures in faraway kingdoms are all very well, but it is still important to be tucked into one's own bed at night. So the susceptible heart of the child perceives the possibility for heroism even in the everyday world of personal experience.

Psychologist Frank Farley investigated young people's perceptions of heroes and identified four dimensions that characterize heroes. Elizabeth Stark summarizes his yet unpublished research in an article in *Psychology Today* (1986). Farley calls the first of his factors, *determinence*; this factor is composed of courage, generosity, expertise, and affection. Since these are heroes of everyday long-term relationships, it is not surprising that the second dimension, *depth*, implies that the hero stands up to the test of time; the child's heroes behave consistently for a dependable period. The third dimension is *distance*. It is important that the child feels close to the hero and has a strong sense of the heroic presence. Seen up close, heroism does not need to be so grand; the need to traverse the distance between hero and observer is what calls for larger action. The fourth dimension is *domain*, the arena in which the hero excels. Here again, choice may be partly determined by how familiar the hero's territory is, how easy it is for the child to picture herself in the heroic location. But another influence may also be at work. The hero may represent access to a domain the young person aspires to rather than the one she actually inhabits.

A later article describes Farley's theory of heroism as having *five* traits, the four already named and a fifth: data base. *Data base* refers to where people have learned about their heroes: at school, from books, movies, television, and radio (Buffington, 1989).

Farley asked elementary school students and college students to name their heroes. Both groups overwhelmingly named their parents. As to gender differences, Farley found that girls and women were more likely than boys and men to name their parents as heroes. And while men named "glamour figures" like Madonna and Marilyn Monroe (perhaps confusing attraction with heroism), women's lists included feminists like Jane Fonda, Susan B. Anthony, and Geraldine Ferraro.

The difference between these two types of women heroes—Madonna versus Susan B. Anthony—reveals more than the difference between the shallow and the substantial. It also echoes Farley's point about distance: boys see images of women rather than actual women doing heroic things. This split also summarizes the dilemma of some modern women. Although the everyday characters of these women's childhoods are exemplary and admirable, our culture doesn't recognize commonplace heroism. Too often women who want a definition of heroism to accompany them in their public interactions limit themselves to models who have gained wide social recognition. This squanders the heroic behavior that could fruitfully be translated from the familiar scenes of childhood. Courage, determination, and persistence are heroic qualities whether they are used in managing a household or in the halls of Congress.

Women in the 1960s, 1970s, and 1980s who took their part in the larger battles of the world were spiritually the daughters of "ordinary" nonheroic women. Women in the 1940s learned from the domestic ingenuity and indomitability of their mothers and grandmothers. What they learned gave them courage as they ferried airplanes into combat zones, carried out secret and subversive actions against the enemies, hid endangered people, and filled the jobs that men had left behind. In 1991, the daughters and granddaughters of these generations of women asserted their right to move even more directly into battle in the Persian Gulf War.

One of the common surprises in therapy is when a woman discovers that a quality her mother displayed being *"just* a wife and mother" turns out to have surprising application in her own career life. One woman realized, for example, that the dexterity and integrity her mother used in balancing the demands of an autocratic husband with raising her children according to her own ideals were traits that served the patient well in managing the editorial staff of a large professional publication.

The Heroes of Adolescence

The perspective of childhood serves as a basis for the heroic ideals that animate adult behavior. But in adolescence the perspective broadens: from lessons learned from parents and fairy tales to the interactions of the expanded everyday world.

In adolescence, although still concerned with their ability to meet and overcome difficulty, teenagers become preoccupied with finding out who they are and how their peers and special adults see them. Teenagers have more or less mastered the challenges of childhood that were dominated by domestic concerns. As they move into the world of contemporaries, they are painfully concerned with how they stand with their fellows.

This is a touchingly hero-inspired time. Adolescents try to walk or talk like their heroes. They practice being tough, inscrutable, or glamourous. Adolescents are beginning to assume a community larger than their families. They disagree with parents or teachers, whom they see as old-fashioned, clumsy, and overbearing. The adolescent is fascinated by a series of heroes who provide a temporary sense of self that can be shed like the too-tight skin of the snake.

I remember one teenager, a patient, who went through a painful time because she felt awkward and her way of relating to other people was argumentative and troublesome. The first time we met, she paused at the door of my office, held her purse at arm's length, paused, dramatically said, "You're the seventh shrink I've seen," and dropped her purse. Impressed, I said, "What an entrance!" It turned out to be just what she wanted to hear. Our subsequent work together, while not free of turmoil, rested firmly on my respect for her style. My recognition of her own heroic struggle for identity—and her dramatization of it—made her willing to relate to me too as the individual I was, not merely a representative of adult authority. Her adolescence was a turning point in the diary of her personal development. She was in the early stage in the struggle against limitations, where people push out against a confining status quo. Throughout history, heroes have typified the human attempt to expand present abilities into new levels of skill or application. This struggle is especially perceptible in the tender self of the adolescent.

The Heroes of Societies

Legendary heroes were celebrated in mythology because they personified the qualities a given society wanted its citizens to emulate. In the past, as we have seen, the heroic example promoted allegiance to the standards of conduct the community required. Indeed, Ernest Becker (1973, p. 7) has called society "a codified hero system." He proposes that what distinguishes one society from another are the different hero systems that regulate their conduct. Each society has its own hierarchy of heroes, ranging from the influential leader whose behavior affects millions of people to the simple hero who inspires perhaps one other person.

Within this hierarchy of heroic images there is an informal set of rules and ideals reflecting the valued behavior for members of that society. Drawing from this catalogue, each individual then redefines the heroic image (sometimes consciously, sometimes unconsciously), tailoring it to serve her own needs and purposes, to fit her own talents and circumstances. Thus, heroes are agents of change: they move other people—sometimes whole societies—forward with them. Classic legends ring with the durable names of men whose valor changed their times: Achilles, Moses, Odysseus, Samson, Hercules.

Who Are the Heroes for Women?

Biblical and Greek legends are full of the doings of men, with only occasional asides about women. Moses parted the Red Sea so that the children of Israel could pass; Joshua "fit the battle" of Jericho; Achilles and Hector were heroes of the Trojan War. Trumpets, pennants, and glory are theirs. Our contemporary myths are often merely modern versions of the ancient hero tales dressed up in new clothes. Moses, Joshua, Achilles, and Odysseus turn up again as Luke Skywalker, Rambo, Superman, and the Terminator.

Historical records, too, abound with male heroes. We can almost trace our national childhood and adolescence in the parade of men we have adopted as our folk heroes. Additionally, we can see the development of a national mythology popularizing these idols. George Washington, for example, served the colonists' need to transmute treason into an ethical act of independence. He was an indispensible transitional figure between revolution and constitutional self-rule.

It seems clear that young men have a populous gallery of heroes stretching back for centuries, but to whom can a young woman look for inspiration? Her classic models are Penelope, the devoted stay-at-home wife, Cassandra, unheeded prophet and sexual prize of war, Guinevere, Arthur's faithless queen, and Helen of Troy, the beautiful troublemaker.

This lack of inspirational models is not limited to classic tales. Who are the female heroes today? Surely not Lois Lane, whose posturing spunkiness gets her into constant predicaments from which she is then rescued by Superman. Surely not the country's First Lady, who has no governing power and in most cases actually submerges her individual opinions into a homogenized image of agreement. Superwoman? She is just a clone of the male pop hero in a sexy but inefficiently designed outfit.

Who are the women heroes of the American Revolutionary War and the Civil War? Of course, there was the steadfast seamstress, Betsy Ross. But our American history books, as well as a monumental public television series, discuss more completely Civil War generals and their battles than Clara Barton and her equally heroic work. Barton tirelessly organized nursing services for the Civil War's wounded and later founded the American Red Cross.

The names of women who were brave and heroic are only now beginning to appear in our historic hero tales. We learn about Abigail Adams from the opinionated and articulate letters she exchanged with her husband, John Adams, who valued her advice and discussed with her many issues critical to the framing of the Constitution. Abigail Adams participated fully in the rebellious protests of the colonists against British rule. She was wife to one president— the first to live in the White House—and mother of another. For every Abigail whose correspondence was preserved, there were many wives, mothers, and sisters devoted to the colonies' struggle for independence whose identities remain unknown.

The Functions of Heroism

Obviously, heroism can be trivialized and cynically manipulated, especially in an age when the mass production of images and the processing of information operate at full speed. Sleazy images can condition us to disbelieve, to dismiss heroism as mere puffery and its influence as insubstantial. But that is misleading. The concept of heroism has persisted because it is *functional*. It has fascinated countless thoughtful people, each seeking a definitive way to describe this central human impulse.

Thomas Carlyle, in the 1840s, delivered a course of lectures on heroes and described them as "leaders of men . . . the modellers, patterns, and in a wide sense creators, of whatsoever the general mass of men contrived to do or to attain" (1903, p. 1). Joseph Campbell (1973) suggests that the hero provides a boon for his comrades or countrymen, thereby improving the welfare of his community. Henry Murray (1960) defines a hero as a person who has made an important contribution to the foundation, survival, or development of his society. To Farley (Stark, 1986, p. 12), a hero is "someone who does something to make the world better." Eliade (1975) says that mythical heroes remind us that grand events have taken place; identifying with heroes elevates us all.

What *are* these boons, these contributions of heroes that make the world better? Let me propose some.

Transcendence of Time and Space

As far as we know, we are the only animals who establish ourselves along the dimensions of past and future. The future, we know, contains our own death. Becker (1973, p. ix) says that "the idea of death, the fear of it . . . haunts the human animal. . . . It is a mainspring of human activity—activity designed largely to avoid the fatality of death, to overcome it by denying in some way that it is the final destiny for man." In the face of our inevitable end, we search for people who help us stretch beyond personal mortality, who affirm some powerful and immortal elements in our own existence.

Therefore, one of the recurrent themes of heroic exploits is the hero's challenge of death. Orpheus, for example, invades the underworld in order to obtain the return of his beloved Eurydice. Christ raids hell to rescue the virtuous pagans, and Hercules descends into the underworld to free the hero Theseus. Victory over time, as it is represented by a victory over human mortality, is one of the central themes of heroism.

Heroism overcomes time in yet another way: by reminding us of ageless ideals. Heroic individuals connect us to the timeless parade of people who have gone before us and those who will live after us. Women without heroic example are deprived of the ability to think of things outside of their immediate existence. For them, the dimensions of past and future stretch only as far as their individual lifetimes. Many adult women are mired in the present. They live like prisoners serving an indeterminate sentence, knowing only the flat chronology of a personal now. In its most pronounced form, this is depression, the loss of a sense of personal option and effect, a feeling of impotence and alienation from the important business of the world.

Women with no heroes of their own are limited in space as well as time. Fixed in the lonely terrain of their own lives, their actions have a narrow horizon, restricted to a landscape that is limited to their own personal survey. The heroic woman, on the contrary, extends herself into a community of spirit and shared hopes. She inspires other women to see newly available futures, to determine their own geographies.

An example. Arlene, a gifted graduate student, was torn between her studies in the United States and the plight of her mother back in an oppressive country. Arlene tormented herself with questions about whether she should return to her country and share her mother's plight. As we talked, she remembered childhood scenes that demonstrated her mother's wholehearted endorsement of her daughter's studies. Arlene's escape was not felt as abandonment; it actually furthered her mother's heroic dreams that had begun as she watched her bright young daughter grow. Arlene was transcending her mother's tragic restrictions by entering a world where aspiration and acceptance overlooked superficial characteristics. There were *two* heroes in this story: the mother who dreamed of a world larger than she herself knew and the daughter who overcame her own internal doubts to claim her citizenship in such a world.

Another woman I saw in therapy, Leila, remarked to me recently how important a comment of mine had been to her. I had observed that despite an upbringing that stressed not venturing beyond her family's rules and accomplishments, it was both desirable and *inevitable* that Leila should want a better life for herself. Until then Leila had suspected she would be disloyal if she did not remain stuck in the familial time warp. I asked her to imagine that she had a young daughter and to tell *her* what kind of life she could have. The experiences Leila wanted for her daughter were experiences she wanted for herself. While she couldn't have them all, she identified a few that she *could* have: travel, a different job, and more time with her friends. Why wait for these good things to happen to her daughter?

Revelation of the Possible

The heroic woman's spirit speaks to the possible, the as-yet-unrealized potential in *every* woman. This revelation can hearten previously passive women to engage actively in their own cause.

For example, I mentioned previously the woman pilots Amelia Earhart and Beryl Markham. They showed that women had the vision, daring, and stamina to fly solo across vast oceans. Before their flights, the roles of aviator and daredevil were unthinkingly assumed to be exclusively male. But their exploits opened the skies up to other women. Women have been astronauts (Judith Resnick and Sally Ride), have set new world records for flight, and have served as copilots on experimental aircraft (Jeana Yeager on the glider flight around the world). Christa McAuliffe, the teacher who died in the shuttle *Challenger* tragedy, taught us that women, as well as men, demonstrate courage and determination in the face of the unknown.

Exemplifying a Common Dream

One reason we respond to heroes is that they represent more than individual discontent. When a heroic woman confronts an outmoded belief or an unjust practice, she speaks for many women whose dissatisfaction had been vague or inarticulate. When a particular hero questions a prevailing ethos, she identifies policies that have become equally stale and oppressive to other women who either cannot or dare not state their complaint. For example, the women journalists at a convention of the American Society of Newspaper Editors pointed up the lack of women executives and editors in American newspapers (80 of the society's 1,000 members are women). Katherine W. Fanning, the editor of the *Christian Science Monitor*, said, "It was time we vented the issue." These women spoke for all the women with newsroom jobs who aspire to executive desks—but who were not at the meeting (Jones, 1988, p. C32).

The first black child to enter an all-white Southern school represented all the black children who had been turned away. But although black students in other parts of the South took heart from her example, each one of them had to summon courage of her or his own. Each individual confrontation was a fresh challenge.

Sophia Bracy Harris and her sister were the first black children to go to a Wetumpka, Alabama, high school in 1965. Sophia's home was bombed, and she lived with the ostracism and unremitting scorn of students and faculty. But instead of being intimidated, she built from that experience. She worked for passage of a bill mandating day care for low-income families, and she organized the Black Women's Leadership and Economic Development Project to help women get off the welfare rolls and out of dead-end jobs. Sophia remembered the anguish of her high school days and wanted to help others move beyond their own pain: "I'm not talking struggle. Struggle is OK. It's the pain that is wrong" ("Heroes for Hard Times," 1988, p. 26).

Rosa Parks represented the black people who were no longer willing to move to the back of the bus. Marian Anderson's voice sang for all the magnificent voices that had been denied access to the world's concert halls and opera houses. Jackie Robinson represented all the black athletes who had never been allowed to play on major league baseball teams. Every black person elected to Congress demonstrates the right of all black Americans to be there.

And they all know it.

Man: The Standard Hero

When heroism is all male and women's heroism is neither recognized nor celebrated, half of our population is left without example, left to borrow or accept a secondhand heroism that may not suit their talents and inclinations.

Too often, the studies of sexual differences (as we will see in Chapter Four) describe women's behavior as *not* this or that, usually meaning *not* masculine. This leaves women with little but negative images of themselves. For centuries, women have been taught that their role is to be helpful to men and to provide them with unobtrusive support and care. It is not surprising that many women have developed an ingratiating style that does not compete for attention or prominence.

Stereotyping can have ironic complications, even for the dominant group. Men have been discouraged from differing from the male stereotype. When men seek to correct imbalances in their own lives by restoring some of their previously denied feelings, they may find it a difficult task to accomplish (Bly, 1990).

One patient, Gerard, was more fortunate than some. He had been reared in a strict religious tradition that taught that God meted out punishment to mortals, who were inevitably guilty. In his forties, Gerard delivered his own internal sermons, criticizing himself in the same unforgiving manner. One day he said that although he would very much like to be able to pray, he couldn't bring himself to pray to the uncompassionate God of his childhood. When I asked him to visualize the God he *could* pray to, tears filled his eyes and he spoke to a gentler, more attentive divinity. Softly he spoke of his need to be more compassionate with himself, and he asked his God to help him do this. For Gerard to cry was an important move beyond his habitual turn of mind, an entry into a new kind of union with God. But as a consequence he also became more understanding with his colleagues at work and overcame his troublesome sense of alienation from them.

The Pace of Heroism

Most acts deemed heroic are breathtaking, cliff-hanging, and very limited in their span of time. The masculine slant on heroism has led to a concept that conforms to the classic laws of dramatic unity: simple in time, characters, plot, and setting—easy to relate.

It seems more compelling, for example, to report on men climbing a previously unscaled mountain, tallying their progress in inches over treacherous terrain, than to describe the unmeasurable day-to-day struggles of a woman trying to establish a profitable cottage industry in an impoverished mining town. Yet both enterprises require the heroic qualities of vision, courage, stamina, and persistence, along with a generous expenditure of self and energy.

The heroism of women is rooted in events and relationships that do not always fit easily into linear, time-limited scenarios. One woman wrote me, "Women's heroism is heroism in slow-motion." There are so many ways to save a life, and not all of them have captivating instant drama and flash. Where is the attention and respect earned by devoted nurses and dedicated teachers? What of the caretakers of elderly parents or disabled or incompetent siblings?

James Thurber's Walter Mitty was obsessed with heroism. Thurber knew what some of us may be embarrassed to admit: most of us wish to be heroes. Ernest Becker knew this too. He wrote, "The urge to heroism is natural, and to admit it honest. For everyone to admit it would probably release such pent-up force as to be devastating to societies as they are now" (1973, p. 4).

Conclusion

The concept of the hero has endured because it serves a fundamental human need. But to the extent that the definition of heroism is incomplete or skewed, it cannot serve us well. We have been left with a misleading emphasis on physical strength, bravado, and defiant talk and posture. We need to acknowledge the persistent efforts of courageous women who, through quiet patience, noisy argument, direct confrontation, or inventive conciliation, have pursued their heroic visions for generations.

There are basic qualities that characterize all heroes, women or men. We have too long accepted a narrow definition of heroism, rooted in archaic values and ancient needs, that excludes many men, as well as women. We need a redefinition of heroism for our times that incorporates the special qualities that distinguish the heroism of women. Such a definition could humanize the classic heroic image and strengthen its relevance to the whole range of human struggle.

FOUR

Big Boys and Nice Little Girls

I'll get nailed for this, but I feel sorry for men. Our society, current popular psychology to the contrary, seldom wants boys to cry and almost never wants boys to admit to weakness, let alone tenderness. It's not, well, male.
—Linda Ellerbee, *And So It Goes*

The same issue that interests society in general is also a central and provocative question in our look at heroism. Which is more important: heredity or environment, nature or nurture?

This basic concern preoccupies everyone interested in human behavior; the study of these two influences has produced vast libraries of research and thought. No answers are provided here; I offer a brief overview of some provocative observations by people who have explored the question.

We must bear in mind that, although some differences appear inborn, centuries of reinforcement of certain behaviors (and disapproval of others) may have led to a perpetuation of the desired personal characteristics and temperaments and the disappearance of others. Some behaviors we regard as *innate* may have actually been *acquired*, and are thus susceptible to change.

The First Years: Infancy

Human growth has been described as a developmental shift in the balance between environmental support and self-support. The infant, for example, starts out totally dependent on a benign environment merely to survive and then gradually acquires the abilities that make her more and more independent.

Many investigators have studied the influence of babies' physiques and temperaments on their interactions with their environment. To begin with, boys are usually larger at birth than girls, and a greater proportion of their size is composed of muscle (Bardwick, 1971). Infant boys are also described as energetic and active. In one study, the response of three- and four-month-old boys to visual and auditory stimulation was likely to be "twisting and moving about" restlessly, while baby girls responded "to excitement generated by the attempt to assimilate an interesting, or discrepant, event" (Williams, 1987, p. 140).

At birth girls are developmentally older than boys by four to six weeks as measured by the shape and hardness of their bones (Williams, 1987). Although girls appear more reactive to their surroundings than do boys, their reactivity is less overtly physical. Girls remain interested in their environment longer, their attention span is greater, but their interaction is predominately visual rather than tactile. They look, but they are slower to reach for or touch objects (Bardwick, 1971).

Childhood

At nursery school age, boys more frequently grab toys, fight with other children, and defy adult requests. They appear more likely to overlook what they decide is meaningless to their goals, to be more intent on their own purposes, and to struggle against parental pressure in order to achieve their independence (Bardwick, 1971).

As they mature, boys' self-esteem is more and more based on tangible results, on achievements that can be measured, counted, and then tallied up. Gilligan (1982) observes that boys' games are more likely to be those where there are clearly defined rules and they can keep score.

Another early difference between boys and girls is that girls less often strike other children. Although girls may indeed behave as aggressively as boys, their aggressive behavior (predictive of adulthood) is more likely to be verbal than physical. Girls more often try to persuade than to overpower. Their challenges are more likely to take the form of criticism, scolding, and gibes. This preference can come from early experiences as well as genetic endowment. The little girl may have tried a direct exercise of raw power and lost to a more aggressive and experienced little boy. Win or lose, somebody may have told her that "nice little girls don't fight."

I remember our daughter's first year in kindergarten. She suddenly began backing away from battles with the little boy who had been her playmate for years. Actually, she could still more than hold her own, but her kindergarten teacher was a proper, grandmotherly woman who implanted her traditional ideas about how boys and girls were to behave. Our daughter caught on only too quickly.

Messages about proper behavior for girls and boys are repeated and amplified in many ways. Look at the stories that boys read: countless examples of brave young lads who disobey their mothers, steal the property of a clumsy giant or a band of forty thieves, and go on to fame and wealth in spite of well-meaning admonitions of their cautious elders.

Girls' fairy tales are full of passive and patient heroines whose ultimate liberation comes through someone else's efforts. Princes seek them out through enchanted gardens or with glass slippers; mute, these heroines suffer slander or infidelity; drugged, they sleep until they are discovered and kissed back to life. Brave woodsmen appear and rescue them from wicked wolves when their own eyes could have alerted them to danger and their own wits might have helped them avoid or overcome it.

James Thurber, bless him, reversed this familiar scenario in his revision of Little Red Riding Hood. Thurber's heroine goes no closer than twenty-five feet to the bed, pulls a gun out of her basket, and shoots the wolf. "For even in a nightcap a wolf does not look any more like your grandmother than the Metro-Goldwyn lion looks like Calvin Coolidge" (1945, p. 247).

I remember my own discontent as a teenager when I saw the books for girls on the library shelf. All the energy I felt just didn't seem to fit into stories of tea parties or college proms. Very quickly I moved to the boys' books, where adventure on the high seas and the solution of mysteries gave my teenage energy and imagination greater range. Sherlock Holmes rather than Sue Barton, Junior Nurse, for me! Luckily these "unfeminine" preferences didn't get me into trouble. My parents and teachers evidently trusted the public and school libraries; any book I got through those sources was okay.

There are some benefits for girls. They develop language skills earlier than boys. They do well in school subjects that rely on verbal ability. But another important benefit of talking is that talking can minimize and even replace the need to use force. For one thing, it is a safety valve for the release and expression of negative feelings. In addition, it offers an alternative way of influencing an adversary. Reasoning and persuasion, rather than coercion, become possible.

Our masculine image of heroism hasn't valued articulate men. Heroes are supposed to be strong, silent, and made for action, not introspection. The stereotype of the strong, inarticulate male hero who goes it alone is personified by Sylvester Stallone or Arnold Schwarzenegger. Raw, rugged, and direct physical confrontation is their style.

Women's verbally aggressive behavior, far from being lauded, is often viewed as unattractive (nagging and whining) or unhealthy (passive-aggressive). Women who protest verbally are shrill or bitchy (undeniably an exclusively female term), never heroic. They are fishwives and viragos, not eloquent orators like Demosthenes and William Jennings Bryan.

But women certainly do rise to heights of eloquence. Sojourner Truth, for example, was a magnificent natural orator pleading the cause of abolition and women's rights in the early 1800s:

> That man over there says dat women needs to be helped into carriages and lifted over ditches and to have the best place everywhere. Nobody ever help me into carriages or over mud puddles or gives me a best place—and aren't I a woman? . . . I have plowed and planted and gathered into barns, and no man could head me—and aren't I a woman? . . . If the first woman God ever made was strong enough to turn the world upside down all alone, [women] together ought to be able to get it right side up again, and now they're asking to do it, the men better let em [Lerner, 1979, p. 98].

Women haven't lacked heroic eloquence. They have lacked serious listeners.

As they grow up, girls continue to be more aware of their environment than are boys, and perhaps because of this sensitivity, they become more conforming to environmental influence. People approve when boys are aggressive and independent; they call such behavior spunky. Boys are encouraged to relate to their environment in a challenging manner, mastering and overcoming what's "out there." Girls, on the other hand, are encouraged to base their sense of self-esteem on pleasing others and being compliant. Eve was discouraged from growing up; our society still encourages girls to be "nice little girls."

Adults: Survival Needs and Behavior

It may be no accident that the characteristics exhibited by baby boys at birth exemplify, in miniature, our definition of heroic behavior. Such behaviors must have played an important role in the survival and development of the human race. Just as the behavior of infants and children may reflect the influences of socialization and parental approval or disapproval, some of the traits that seem "natural" for women and men may actually be the result of centuries of reward and punishment.

In prehistoric times, the rewards and punishments for acceptable or unacceptable behavior were doled out by natural forces, harshly and pitilessly. Early humans had to divide chores according to physical aptitude; indeed, their very survival depended on it. Hunting, for example, called for short, quick bursts of speed for the hunter to overtake his prey and club it to death, and men surpass women in this type of speed (Ullyot, 1976). In addition, most men are stronger than most women; so the physical aptitude required for the chase—wielding a heavy club and hauling back the carcass—suited men's abilities.

Women, who bore and nursed children, specialized in chores that could be done with the limited mobility allowed by child-rearing. Their tasks included gathering wild grains and seeds, simple snaring of small animals, softening hides for clothing and blankets, and fashioning containers out of clay or reeds to store food. Chores like these are still considered women's work in some of the simple tribal communities of today.

Tasks had to be distributed pragmatically, according to ability and skill. Slower individuals, such as women, old people, and young children, would have been a liability during the hunt. So they stayed at home and performed other chores; girls sat at the side of the women, perhaps, and boys learned from older men no longer swift or strong enough to hunt but who could prepare the boys for their adult roles.

Women concentrated on the welfare and maintenance of the family or clan. It is possible that women's early talent with language emerged from the prehistoric mother's relationship with those who stayed at home during the day (Dinnerstein, 1976). In these interactions there would have been time and opportunity for talk, time that was missing in the quick, urgent conditions of the hunt.

Women's quiet relational skills would have been based on a sense of responsiveness to other people who "needed" care. While these characteristics were surely crucial to the continued existence of the whole species, they would not have been conspicuous.

The relationship skills of her mate, on the other hand, emerged from cooperative and aggressive activities with his peers and his ability to focus singlemindedly on their prey. Men in primitive communities had to develop principles by which their interactions could be equitably governed. They needed rules of conduct pragmatically devised to first regulate the chase and then to determine the fair division of their catch. Language, when they used it, was emergency language designed to communicate quickly in times of action and danger.

Later on, exploratory, militaristic, industrialized, or acquisitive societies still profited from these traits. Early communities were concerned with ensuring ample resources, moving against hostile neighbors, venturing into and claiming new lands and seas, and defending exclusive territorial rights. Monarchs and strategists required action from their citizens, not contemplation and its possible consequences. So action characteristics were called heroic and honored with medals and riches.

Size and strength governed much of the authoritarian hierarchy and determined how disputes were resolved. Physical strength and prowess determined who had the greatest say in the daily interactions of the tribe. Those members of the clan who could overpower others or were experts at the hunt exercised more influence in management and governance.

The same society that requires its men to be off acquiring wealth or fighting wars to protect it needs its women to stay at home to rear the young. Such a society uses similar methods to encourage and enforce women's conformity to its purposes as it does with men. The society's values will be formally expressed in its laws and informally codified in its hero tales. These values will be supported through a complex system of rewards and punishments.

Community pressures can range from social inconveniences to stiff legal penalties. When an individual straying from the traditional female role is considered mildly eccentric, she is merely laughable. But more severe deviations earn stronger reprisals. Serious transgressions are labeled criminal or dangerous and will incur harsher treatment: threats, ostracism, institutionalization, and even death.

In World War II, a young woman in the United States could choose to join the armed forces. But a man had no such choice. The eligible young man joined or was drafted; he faced stiff penalties and strong disapproval if he avoided his responsibility.

In a country that fights wars, medals are routinely given to men for bravery and warriorlike conduct under fire. For women, recognition has sometimes taken a different form. For example, during World War II many American families hung little starred flags in their front windows announcing they had sons in the armed forces. If a son was killed, a flag with a gold star was hung, and the woman of the household was known as a Gold Star Mother.

In this same war, women were also, for the first time, admitted to the armed services. But their participation in active battle was expressly prohibited, though secretly carried out, as we shall see. Today, women in the armed services are taking their place on fields of combat. Sometimes they work side by side with their male comrades in arms; sometimes they work predominantly with women. In both situations women are proving they can perform as well as their male colleagues.

As I have noted, the heroism of women often takes a form other than the exercise of sheer physical power. Heroic women have been expert at verbal contention and audacious thought, at challenging popular belief and practice, and at asking impudent and troublesome questions.

In colonial America, for example, Anne Hutchinson, a powerful "preacher woman" was excommunicated, and one of her supporters, Mary Dyer, was hanged (Chesler, 1972). Hutchinson declared that each individual had a personal responsibility for her own sins and argued that an individual's relationship with God was a direct affiliation; she opposed the mediation of a minister in her communications with God. For her unorthodoxy, Hutchinson was banished from Massachusetts Bay and later died in an Indian massacre along with all but one of her children.

Great rewards can also result from a woman's assertiveness. Elizabeth Freeman ("Mumbet") sued successfully for her freedom from slavery in 1781, citing the Massachusetts Bill of Rights and the state constitution. She had decided that in spite of the common acceptance of the mistreatment and humiliation of her people (or maybe because of it), the principles of freedom applied to her as well as to her masters (DePauw, 1975).

Many heroic women use words. We have already remarked about Harriet Beecher Stowe, whose book *Uncle Tom's Cabin* was thought by many (including, legend has it, Abraham Lincoln) to have been influential in starting the Civil War. Women argue for their cause, like Irene Mack Pyawasit, the first female from her tribe to lobby Congress about Indian problems: "During the time I was there I never allowed the men to even carry my briefcase. I carried my own weight. . . . Sometimes I have to fight alone for an issue . . . it requires me to do a lot of homework so that I know when I open my mouth the words coming out are the right ones. I need to know that the others will understand what I'm saying" (Buss, 1985 p. 163).

Men predominate in formal debates about ethics, governance, and morality—despite women's verbal skills—because women have historically been excluded from public forums and scenes of debate. Women's arguments were often informally made to groups of intimates and remained, therefore, largely unrecorded.

Among the great philosophers we have to listen carefully to hear female voices, but they are there.

Hypatia, a fifth-century teacher and philosopher, fought against the prevailing disapproval of intellectual women and paid for it with her life. She was reputed to be a great scholar of mathematics and philosophy and an inventor of several scientific instruments. Hildegard of Bingen was a twelfth-century prophet and visionary whose prophesies and scientific writings, which included a classification of diseases and medicinal herbs, were widely accepted by monarchs and popes. Hildegard also successfully confronted local church authorities over a disputed burial in the cemetery of the Abbey of Rupertsburg, which she had founded (Walker, 1983; Anderson and Zinsser, 1988a; Warner, 1982).

The belief that women should not speak up is matched by an inhibition against men feeling emotions. Years of burying his feelings may leave a man depressed and unhappily censuring himself because he isn't supposed to feel the way he feels, much less express it. Just think how often little boys are told that "big boys don't cry."

One patient, Stan, had taken this message to heart. Raised by a strict and perfectionistic father, he continued this familiar pattern in an incessant critical self-appraisal. He was also overly critical of members of his family and was repeating the same harsh pattern with his own son. And yet when he would talk about his cold childhood or when he described his ambivalence about his interaction with his son, his eyes would fill with tears and he would feel a tenderness he didn't know how to express because he had stifled it for so long. With his daughter, he could be more tender. After all, she was a girl, and so she was outside the harsh regulations that govern male interaction. In therapy one evening, Stan went back in fantasy to a painful time with his father; he imagined how he would have liked to have been talked to, and he spoke softly of how important it was to try and keep trying, even though you might not do as well as you would like. Good message, both for himself and for his children.

Technology and Sex Differences

Technology has made it possible to rethink roles once simply a matter of biology. It has released an impartial flow of information, although access to some of this information may still be inequitably controlled. But it has done much more.

Technology has increased women's options about childbearing, and it has freed women from constant and exclusive attendance on their children and their household tasks. Women now have the power of decision in areas that previously did not offer a lot of choice. And choice, the possibility to determine one's own future, often confronts a woman with heroic options.

Another profound consequence of technology is that it has virtually revolutionized traditional sex roles by providing an unbiased source of mechanical energy. Technology made it possible (and war made it necessary) for women to invade the defense factories and other heavy industries during World War II. Even though women had to clear out of the factories after the war in order to vacate jobs for the returning veterans, the relationship between women, men, and machinery was never the same. Like the familiar story of the genie in the bottle, it was relatively easy to get the genie out of the bottle, but it's been quite another matter to get her back into it. For better or worse, we all know now that women are able to do many a "man's job."

Necessity has always been an equal opportunity employer. Women have worked side by side with their husbands and families in the fields, at the harvests, in the small shops and businesses of developing urbanization; many of them still do. But now more and more industrial work is done by computers and robots. Pressing a button on a washing machine or operating mechanical devices in their homes has taught women that they can also press buttons on a drill press or operate a riveting machine. The muscular strength that previously marked certain occupations as male and that kept women out of enterprises of heroic scope and vision just doesn't dominate as it once did. Dexterity, endurance, and intelligence are qualifying skills in our technological age; here women are just as capable as men.

The computer is a resoundingly important development of technology and is even more valuable than it appears at first glance. It is a modern sorcerer's apprentice. It is a more neutral piece of machinery than a riveting machine; it spews out information at the slightest touch of a finger, and it doesn't care whether the inquiry comes from a woman or a man. Like other instruments that are operated from a seated position (from spinets to sewing machines), it feels more sympathetic than other machines when it is used by a woman. We have grown accustomed to seeing women seated at typewriters. The typewriter, along with the telephone switchboard, is the modern equivalent of a harpsichord or a spinning wheel. Imagine, any woman can buy a computer and tap into stores of data—much better than Pandora's box or Eve's apple.

Technology in the home has considerably influenced the delineation of the different worlds of women and men. Appliances are ostensibly marketed to make the chores of the housewife easier, but a closer look shows otherwise. Some household technology has actually increased the separation of women's and men's activities because women's co-workers became machines rather than the men who had formerly done the duties of "husbanding" their households (Cowan, 1983). Furthermore, the complexity of household machines virtually ensures that the housewife must call in an out-of-house expert who knows how to repair them, which results in further specialization.

Paradoxically, because of interest in the newest and latest appliance, the housewife now performs many tasks within her home that might better be delegated to someone outside the home. With a rented machine she may feel she should sand her own floors; her neighborhood paint store makes painting her walls seem so easy it's sluggardly not to do it herself. Worse than that, many working women are still made to feel that they are supposed to do it all, to be both career and domestic Superwomen (Shaevitz, 1984).

For many women, household technology has taken on a symbolic function. As more and more women took jobs outside the home and felt guilty about leaving their traditional scene, they came to need reassurance that they were not shirking their traditional female roles. For some women, guilt took the place of simple competence and generosity. So they began baking their own bread, raising their own vegetables, and giving homemade gifts at Christmas.

Meg is a classic example. She works part time and drives her two young children to school and to their after-hours activities. She describes her hectic schedule as "always being late for everything." Nevertheless, when it came time to bake some holiday cookies for her son's class, she felt guilty because she only had time to make two different kinds of cookies instead of four!

Marketing technology has been quick to capitalize on this type of guilt. Now we find the "luxury" appliances that help the working woman (supposedly more affluent) compensate for supposedly shirking her duties: the automatic breadmaker, for example, and the ice cream machine. She need not have worried about shirking her responsibilities; statistics show that in a two-career household the woman still is responsible for most of the housekeeping chores. Statistics also show that most women work out of economic necessity. The appliances they *can* afford are aimed at helping them with some essential household chores; they have neither the time nor the energy to make homemade ice cream.

Conclusion

The same children who seem so impressionable are actually unique little systems of built-in predispositions and talents that shape *how* they conform. Our ideas about heroism are superimposed on some very important individual and gender differences. Not only do women and men differ from each other; women differ from other women and men from other men. When Samuel Johnson was asked whether men or women were more intelligent, he replied, "Which man, which woman?" (Williams, 1987, p. 173).

Some differences between the sexes appear so early that it does not seem unreasonable to speculate that they may have a genetic origin. But such behaviors are also very susceptible to environmental influence. For example, every child is capable of learning any of the world's languages. But children end up speaking the language of their own culture; the sounds and patterns of other languages do not develop.

Society's conceptions of the "proper" contributions and behavior of women and men may make it difficult to uncover actual historical occurrences. For example, historians searching through the yellowed lists of petitioners, canvassers, signatories, and contributors to political causes have found that men were individually listed. But they uncovered few women's names. Even though women participated, their names and actions were subsumed under the family name, and they themselves were not identified as individuals (Lerner, 1979; Anderson and Zinsser, 1988b).

This oversight reflects the social protocol of the times. It does not mean that women couldn't or didn't participate; it suggests that women's contributions were seen as different from the more direct interaction that seemed "natural" for men.

From what we read in the diaries of homesteading women of the United States, it seems safe to assume that the dramatic but anonymous dedication of women has occurred throughout history, whether it was recorded or not. But, historically, women have not been encouraged to emerge from the background, where good little girls belonged.

FIVE

Knowledge and Innocence

*Be plain in dress, and sober in your diet; In short, my deary,
kiss me, and be quiet.*
> —Lady Mary Wortley Montagu,* *Essays
> and Poems and Simplicity, a Comedy*

John Milton, in *Paradise Lost*, voices the uneasiness of men of his
times. His Eve speculates about whether she should share the apple
with Adam or keep it—and the knowledge it conferred—for herself,
thus becoming "more equal, and perhaps/A thing not undesirable,
sometimes/Superior, for inferior, who is free?" (1935, p. 299).

The specter of a knowledgeable woman, well-informed and
thinking independently, responsible for making decisions and carrying them out, has haunted traditional male precincts for centuries. Even now, in this age of supposed enlightenment, this fear
continues to limit women in the modern worlds of scholarship,
science, and business.

Worse, these misgivings have often seeded self-doubt in
women themselves. They fear that being knowledgeable makes
them undesirable. Anna Quindlen (1990, p. A19) reports that a
smart thirteen-year-old girl told her, "Boys don't like it if you
answer too much in class." This is a shrewd conclusion. In her own

---

*Lady Mary Wortley Montagu was herself not a quiet woman. She cam-
paigned energetically and successfully for an effective inoculation against
smallpox in 18th-century England in the face of vigorous medical and
religious opposition. She was described as having "a tongue like a viper
and a pen like a razor" (Vare and Ptacek, 1988, p. 208).

way, this teenager has summarized what social psychologists have found in scientific research. A study conducted by Carli turned up this tidbit of information: men are more likely to change their minds in response to a woman who speaks tentatively than to a woman who is direct and assertive (Bass, 1991).

Clever Men, Innocent Women

Knowledge takes many forms: cleverness, mastery, sexual savvy, intelligence, understanding, and expertise. For men to be clever is a common standard. The male hero who answers questions that have stumped others or who outsmarts bullies who threaten beautiful women is applauded in countless tales. Tailors, shoemakers, princes, and sages unravel the mysteries of haughty princesses, create ingenious strategies to confront arrogant tyrants, and cunningly destroy awesome monsters. Oedipus answered the riddle of the Sphinx and rid Thebes of the plague. David, with his simple slingshot, cleverly felled his outsize opponent, the giant Goliath. Each contest was serious; failure could have resulted in the hero's death or in the continued tyranny of a monster.

On the other end of this cultural IQ scale, ancient legends celebrate women's *innocence*, not their knowledge. Although women are not themselves acceptable as heroic figures, they do very well as human bargaining chips, used to appease or intercede with unpredictable and touchy gods. In such divine bargaining, the ancients reasoned that the sacrifice had to be as attractive as possible so the gods would be pleased with the petitioners. One way to ensure acceptability was to assume that what pleased them would also please their gods. So they would look for flawless flowers, grains, animals, and humans. Virginity, symbolizing both the unworldliness and the intact perfection of the human sacrificial offering, was an obviously attractive characteristic.

Ritual adoration and sacrifice of virgins demanded female purity characterized by sexual innocence and the lack of any serious adult learning. The sacrificially prized girl was carefully guarded and explicitly prohibited from acquiring sexual experience, which was symbolically equated with worldly knowledge.

In ancient Peru, for example, a young girl was "married" to

a sacred stone. After the marriage, she vowed eternal chastity and dedication to the service of the god this stone represented. On other sacred occasions young girls, covered with garlands and treated with great reverence, were thrown into rivers as "brides" for river spirits or water gods. Their sacrificial death would procure ample irrigation and a generous harvest (Frazer, 1949).

Virginal innocence, like Eve's abstinence from the tree of knowledge of good and evil, called for women to reject both sexual and intellectual maturity. Warner (1985, p. 64) observes that "virginity's principal attraction is its ability to cancel woman's womanliness." Canceling out her womanliness obviously implies that whatever personal authority the young woman might exert would also be canceled.

Mistrust and Mystification as Explanation

Primitive people probably found the phenomena of conception and childbirth as impressive as all the other natural wonders that confronted them. To them, women were magical containers from which other miniature human beings emerged.

As long as men didn't fully understand the mechanics of conception, this apparently exclusively female process could make them wonder uneasily about what other mysterious capacities women might possess. Just as they explained storms at sea by ascribing godlike and intentional malevolence to angry winds or aggrieved oceans, primitive men tried to explain their own sexual attraction to their fertile childbearing comrades. Men's impulses were attributed to the magical powers of women. Female guile was to blame; women were not to be trusted. (The contemporary version of this projection of blame is the rapist's defense that the victim behaved or dressed provocatively and "brought it on herself.")

In addition to pregnancy and birth, women had other characteristics that mystified their male comrades. The menstrual cycle, for example, was for centuries an object of superstitious and ritualistic dread in men. Just imagine the wonder of primitive men at seeing this bloody discharge. In their experience—the slaughter of animals or the wounds of their companions in battle—a flow of blood meant almost certain death. And yet in women this flow was a regular and predictable event that stopped only to give way to the equally awesome act of giving birth and then resumed. These were female mysteries of the first order, and they invited all the inventive explanations that men could muster—and invent they did.

The mystery and fear surrounding menstruation and conception have found expression in countless customs, beliefs, and taboos that reveal men's ambivalent fascination with the fertility of women and their attempt to dominate it. The snake, who would shed its skin, apparently die, then emerge again as if reborn, became a symbol for fertility. It is not surprising that Eve's conspiratorial ally was a snake. Women's easy communication with snakes, like Eve's and like that of Greek priestesses and oracles, was seen as beneficial when used for healing or ominous when used in witchcraft.

The early Romans warned of the dire effects a menstruating woman had on seeds, wine, grass, and fruit trees (Bardwick, 1971). In some present-day primitive societies, menstruating women are confined together in a special hut until their periods are over. And as recently as the late nineteenth century, medical advice quaintly recommended that women avoid intellectual activity during menstruation since it might "cause an imbalance due to an oversupply of blood flowing toward the brain instead of downward" (Reese, Wilkinson, and Koppelman, 1983, p. 25).

The subordination of women was a gradual process. The earliest attitude toward women's fertility was one of awe and reverence. Female goddesses were worshipped, and the metaphoric relationship of female fecundity to the fertility of the earth arose. Phillips (1984, p. 3) proposes, indeed, that Eve is best understood "as a deposed Creator Goddess." Other writers have speculated that the earliest divinities may have been female, dethroned by more warlike and aggressive male gods (Graves, 1966; Monaghan, 1981; Stone, 1976). Having Eve born out of Adam is a dramatic early statement, a classic inversion of the procreative power of women and an implicit denial of the divinity of female deities.

Men created gods who, not surprisingly, mirrored their own needs and temperaments. Gods arose who were jealous, wary of powerful women, and dominating. The God of the Old Testament was a father, a patriarch who could create a universe, battle dragons like Leviathan and Tehom, and whose worship was dominated by men. Zeus supplanted Hera in ancient Greece, and the two were thereafter constantly at odds (Monaghan, 1981). Hera, powerful as she was, became a classic nagging wife with a philandering spouse.

A variation on the theme of the knowledgeable woman is the woman-as-mystery, unknown and unknowable. The Lady of the Lake, for example, remains invisible and silent as she hands Arthur the scabbard that will hold his wondrous sword, Excalibur.

As mystical and wise, women symbolically represent the "totality of what can be known" (Campbell, 1973, p. 116). Campbell writes poetically of "the hero with a thousand faces" who searches for this totality, but it's always a male hero who engages in this single-minded quest. The hero's idealized union with this distant and legendary female figure is to make *him* wise and whole. In spite of the woman's indispensability in such myths, her role as reward or accessory is familiar. Woman's mystery is, once again, subsidiary to the man's quest. What the union might offer her is nowhere taken into account.

Imposed Innocence

From their mystic fear of the power of women—and their need to master this power—men developed a mythology and a theology advocating that women were to remain under male control, secluded and contained. Even so, men must have sensed that this was an uneasy arrangement at best. Liveliness in women, although attractive, might have seemed an implicit abrogation of their subordinate position, leading them to trespass into male strongholds.

So numerous legends tell of women tested in provocative situations; they can either prove their virtue by choosing to remain ignorant or provoke disaster when they don't. Pandora is given a jar and then told that she is not to open it under any circumstances. The result? Generations are plagued by the woes released by her disobedience and curiosity. Rapunzel is locked into a tower with no exits, only a window through which she can look at a world she is not permitted to enter. There she waits patiently for the heroic prince (free to roam the world) who rescues her.

Psyche is forbidden to know her husband's name or even look on his face; he visits her only in darkness. Elsa is not to ask her husband, Lohengrin, his name. Both lose their husbands when they dare to inquire into what seems reasonable information a wife might want from her husband. Elsa never is reconciled with Lohengrin—he sails off on the next swan—and Psyche is reunited with her husband only after she endures long struggles and performs arduous tasks assigned by her jealous mother-in-law, Aphrodite.

Bluebeard's wife is a happy exception. She is given keys to certain rooms and then told to never unlock the doors or enter the rooms. But *she* defies the command and, with the assistance of her sister Anne, saves her own life.

The cautionary message in Eve's story is further reinforced by the tradition that she had an evil predecessor. In an early story of the creation, the first woman was Lilith, ungovernable and rebellious right from the beginning (Graves and Patai, 1966). God actually created Eve as a more obedient replacement—poor planning that. But the myth of Lilith still persists, the image of a restless spirit who tauntingly enters the dreams of men. And to make her seem even more villainous. Lilith is also reputedly a danger to newborn infants (Walker, 1983).

Just as heroes typified the values a society wanted in its men, villainous women exemplified the behaviors a society would not condone in its women. In myths and folklore, unmanageable women, painted as villains who came to bad ends, outnumber disobedient men.

These legends tell of the pain that women courted, whether victims or villains, when they even considered moving beyond the confines to which society limited them. When women dared to investigate or inquire into restricted knowledge, they were pictured as unruly, duplicitous, and untrustworthy. The wonder is that so many women continued to defy prohibitions. Natural curiosity dies hard.

For men, however, legendary prohibitions to curiosity are challenges to be heroically overcome. Men's curiosity is not only natural, it is the prelude to great accomplishments. Arthur pulls Excalibur from the rock, thereby demonstrating that he is the once and future king. Jason steals the Golden Fleece, Jack climbs the beanstalk to wealth, Ali Baba follows the forty thieves into the treasure cave. Nobody tells *them* they are to submit to restrictive injunctions. Of course, their actions are not without risk. But often the very act of confronting barriers is what is most admired and what actually qualifies them as heroes.

It is important to remember that some individuals are considered villains precisely because they challenge the prevailing cultural norms and question the previously unquestioned rules. When they do this, they may have a large (but silent) constituency. Villains, not unlike heroes, often represent a sizeable number of individuals who are afraid or unwilling to express their own opposition to popular values. In many cases, the distinction between villainy and heroism depends on the vantage point of history. Many a villain to one group of people is a hero to another. Delilah, after all, was a heroine to the Philistines. It may be that if *they* had written our Bible we should have seen her as such. It is the winner who determines who the heroes and villains are; when one opposes the status quo and loses, fate does not accord the loser a minority report on the conflict.

The Uses of Docility

As primitive societies developed into more complex communities, women's docility turned out to have more than one advantage for men. The powerful commandments regulating female monogamy and marital fidelity, enforced by a sentence of death against adulterers, had economic utility in acquisitive and wealth-based societies because the regulations assured the safe disposition of a man's estate to his legitimate heirs.

When the woman was seen as wise or expert, she might be cast as an invaluable source of aid or information for the male hero. The knowledgeable woman served acceptably as a helper to the heroic man, pointing out directions, helping him acquire certain talismans or amulets, and instructing him in specific skills that would prove useful to him along his way. She might be a beautiful young woman or an old crone. She might possess great artistry and insight or just a simple skill that precisely fit the situation.

Ariadne, for example, made her cleverness useful to Theseus. She showed him how to find his way back out of the labyrinth by unwinding a spool of thread as he entered and simply rewinding it on his way out after he had killed the man-eating Minotaur. Medea helped Jason pilfer the Golden Fleece by using her magic spells to help him get past the soldiers and the guardian dragon.

The legendary alliance between hero and female helper is often only temporary. One of them grows weary or is eager for a new relationship (like Jason) or has specified from the outset that the association is only temporary (like Lady Lyne to Sir Gawain, one of King Arthur's knights). Even the perfect knight, Lancelot, moves on after he is healed and leaves Elaine, the-not-quite-fair-enough.

So although Dido sheltered Aeneas during his long and weary return from the Trojan War, Aeneas deserts her when he remembers that he is destined to found the Roman empire. Ariadne flees with Theseus after betraying her country by helping him defeat the Minotaur, but Theseus abandons her as she sleeps. Years after the adventure of the Golden Fleece, in which Medea was crucial to his success, Jason plans to take their two young sons with him to his new marriage, to a woman who can be more useful to him on his way up the social ladder. Medea's homicidal revenge, killing their two sons and murdering Jason's new bride, has branded her a vile and unnatural mother. But Jason and his Argonauts continue to serve as models of heroism and enterprise.

Repeatedly these myths suggest that a woman is never equal to the man she assists and that she should not aspire to heroic status. Woman's main role in the heroic saga is limited to that of helpful informant, evil villain, innocent victim, unblemished sacrifice, or victor's prize.

The Myth of Untrustworthy Women

Greek tales of bravery and courage were originally sung or recited aloud by professional bards at banquets attended by warriors, leaders, and aristocrats or at the fireside during military campaigns. These stories served important purposes. The Greek myths celebrated the male ancestors of the noble military listeners and also applauded the compliant and supportive cooperation of their women. The ominous image of the knowledgeable woman, who might have wishes of her own, embodied the worst fears of the aggressive men. The warriors had to be assured that women would not distract them from their martial directions or betray them when they were away at war.

So the didactic function of myths evolved to instruct women in desirable behavior. It was instructive to show an evil (obviously cautionary) version of the wise woman: fearsome, cunning, devious, and treacherous. Her gifts, awesome and magical, changed without warning or explanation.

She could be enchantingly beautiful, like Circe, who transformed her guests, homeward-bound veterans of the Trojan War, into swine. Or she could be like the Sirens, whose ethereal songs lured these same warriors to crash their boats on the rocks while they listened. Morgan le Fay, the implacable enemy of King Arthur, cast innumerable spells, deceiving him and bewitching his knights with false and illusory visions. Her malevolent influence led to the downfall of the Round Table and of Camelot itself by turning the knights against each other.

Evil women could be beautiful, like Delilah, who used her beauty to subdue Samson, the great Hebrew hero. But beauty was not the only feminine quality that was mistrusted. Ugliness was suspect, too. The poverty and repugnant appearance of old and deformed women in the sixteenth and seventeenth centuries made them fair game for distrust and suspicion. Scores of old and disfigured women were burned or tortured as witches. Such executions were often based on the old argument that women were morally inferior and susceptible to influence by the devil or his cohorts (Fraser, 1984). Eve's association with the serpent was a familiar accusation that justified continued mistrust.

This bias seems an almost logical development from the earlier tradition of women as prophets. In Greece, the gift of prophecy was granted to certain women, sometimes as recompense for their having taken vows of chastity, sometimes as the result of a liaison with a god. Women's gift of prophecy was also well-known in the Bible; Miriam prophesied the birth and eventual greatness of her brother, Moses, and Rachel prophesied the birth of her second son.

There is a cautionary note, however, in the stories of some of these remarkable women: they also suffered unpleasant consequences. The Trojan princess Cassandra prophesied accurately, but no one believed her. To this day her name is synonymous with disregarded prophecies of doom. When Miriam dared to criticize Moses' relationship with his wife, Jehovah punished her by afflicting her with leprosy (Friedman, 1987). Rachel did indeed give birth to a second son, but she died in childbirth (Monaghan, 1981).

The custom of prophecy continued into the seventeenth century. During the Middle Ages, women who presumed to speak out on matters of religion and conscience were accepted for a while as genuine prophets—but only within tolerable limits. When they got too noisy or too troublesome they were tried and punished, sometimes as common scolds, who were "by definition female" (Fraser, 1984, p. 103). A more serious accusation was directed against those women who preached a message that was unwelcome to the reigning class; they became suspect as associates of the devil and were vulnerable to condemnation as witches.

For example, in 1589 James I of England was waiting for his bride to come from Denmark. Princess Anne was delayed for months by stormy seas. James, certain this delay was caused by witches' spells, had many unfortunate women executed. In America in 1692, the witchcraft trials of Salem—where innocence was virtually impossible to establish—were a colonial version of European practice. Suspected witches were placed in a "dunking stool" and lowered into deep water. If they drowned they were innocent. But if they floated they were obviously in league with the devil. Young girls, overcome by tales of voodoo told to them by a West Indian slave and perhaps inspired by preacher Cotton Mather's rabid sermons against witchcraft, wildly accused innocent townspeople of being witches. In that year, over one hundred people were either executed as witches or sent to prison.

Knowledge, Responsibility, and Choice

Knowledge is clearly key to power. Reluctance to give up information is rooted in the fear that it will result in loss of power as well. Many women still find that they have to dig hard to get some of the same information that is passed around easily among men in the same organizations. Casual exchanges of vital news often occur in leisure activities and private settings that exclude women. The apple tree is not only prohibited; it is fenced off or concealed.

Even so, knowledge is easier to come by today. One benefit of the technological advances in communication and data processing is that access to information is democratized. Women cannot be kept uninformed as easily as before. Our data-rich society has given women what Eve discovered to be a paradoxical gift, and the potential heroism of contemporary women has been expanded by women's increased opportunity to make informed choices.

The heroic awareness of choice has always carried with it an equally sharp awareness of the dangerous consequences. Heroic women risk the safety and comfort of the status quo when they assert their intelligence, their right to know, and their right to self-determined action. Nowadays women are less likely to risk death in making their heroic choices, but sometimes the risk is isolation or scorn. In primitive societies, of course, derision could lead to physical injury and ostracism could mean death. Even in "civilized" societies, for some women independent choice may result in such disapproval that it becomes almost a death sentence during their lifetime.

Florence Nightingale is a prime example of a woman who chose to diverge from the conventional path for a woman of her upbringing. Very different from the genteel cardboard figure she has become, Florence chafed under the accepted standards for well-bred Englishwomen: "What am I that their [other women's] life is not good enough for me? Oh God, what am I? . . . Why, oh my God, cannot I be satisfied with the life that satisfies so many people? I am told that the conversation of all these good clever men ought to be enough for me. Why am I starving, desperate, diseased on it?" (Anderson and Zinsser, 1988b, p. 167). Instead of accepting her comfortable and safe life, she mystified and shocked her contemporaries by choosing to walk the grim corridors of army hospitals half a world away.

Ridicule and jeers didn't dissuade Susan B. Anthony from her crusade for women's suffrage. She persevered in lecturing and petitioning the legislators who had the power to correct the inequity. Pictures of these two women show them as so prim, in their modest nineteenth-century dress. But their visions went way beyond lace collars and cameos.

There is still great pressure on women to "earn" their protected and cherished status by accepting a role of ignorance and limited relevance. If women live up to their part of the bargain, society will, in turn, maintain and defend the offered benefits as well as the imposed restrictions. We have already met Darlene, who pursued her heroic struggle to get a practical education in spite of her abusive husband. Here she is, Eve's daughter indeed, challenging herself to be equal: "for inferior, who is free?" as Milton's Eve asks.

Women in Science

Women's participation in technology remains slight. A look through the employment and earnings data for 1990 shows that men outnumber women by a ratio of at least two to one in such positions as mathematical and computer scientists and natural scientists (U.S. Department of Labor, 1991). The same survey reveals that women are also less likely to be found in management positions. Women are also outnumbered as engineers.

These data tell us more than the unsurprising news that women have historically not entered certain fields. The deeper significance is that women are exercising little influence in shaping the technology that these sciences will introduce into our lives, from relatively simple refrigerators to complex nuclear power plants.

Curiosity, knowledge, ambition, and personal choice continue to be troublesome characteristics for women. For example, somewhere along the way in their education, girls learn that physics, chemistry, engineering, geology, metallurgy, astronomy, biology, zoology, and other "hard" sciences (to say nothing of statistics, architecture, and math) are not for them. Girls succumb to indirect pressure that implies that any girl interested or competent in these subjects is unfeminine or odd, or both. I still remember the wonder aroused by one of my women colleagues in graduate school because she wrote her dissertation on *statistics*!

This pressure hits hardest in adolescence, a particularly vulnerable time for girls. Initial differences between girls and boys in subjects like the physical sciences actually increase as students move through their school years (Freiberg, 1991).

One young woman who had been raised in the South told me

how she had learned to act demure and to subdue her natural liveliness. As she put it, she was "raised to attract a husband, and
everybody knew that a smart-alecky woman would be passed over."
But now, she wants to change a relationship that was maintained
for years on those terms. Still, old habits die hard, and she has had
to overcome her timidity and her doubts that she can take care of
herself. Sometimes you can hear the echoes of her childhood admonitions as she derides her own wishes, calling them "romantic."

What qualifies one sex for scientific work and disqualifies
the other? Science and technology are assumed to be the exclusive
province of men even though most of these specialties don't require
superior physical strength; brawn is immaterial. In fact, some of the
qualities in which women excel—endurance, persistence, attention
to fine detail, dexterity, awareness of context—are actually advan-
tageous to scientific investigation.

And yet the bias against women in science is widespread.
Biologist Evelyn Shaw discussed her research plans with a male
colleague: "He listened carefully, liked my premise and methodology and then with superb aplomb, carefully shaking out his already
emptied pipe, he turned to me and said, 'You know, you think like
a man. You will become a good scientist'" (1985, p. 36). This man
praised Shaw's ability to think "scientifically," to maintain an unbiased perspective and to distance herself from her investigation so
that her observations would be reliable. The contradiction of his
damning her sex while praising her principles evidently escaped
him.

This anti-female prejudice was clearly expressed in the late
sixteenth century. Francis Bacon attacked his society's superstition,
crude reasoning, and preoccupation with making gold from base
metal. Bacon scorned these occult and alchemical endeavors and
developed a body of sound and consistent principles to govern
scientific investigation. Bacon proposed a metaphor: Intellect was
masculine and Nature was feminine, and the proper endeavor of
science was a "chaste and lawful marriage between Mind and Nature." In Bacon's view, knowledge was power and could lead to the
salvation of mankind. Not surprisingly then, it "became the responsibility of men to assume and exercise that power" (Keller 1985,
pp. 31–33).

Women's interest in scientific knowledge was mistrusted. Woman was like Nature: she was to be controlled and tamed. She was an object to be examined, but she was not allowed to be an active participant in the search for knowledge. More than three hundred years later, this theme was reiterated by Joseph Campbell: "The mythical marriage with the queen goddess of the world represents the hero's total mastery of life; for the woman is life, the hero is its knower and master" (1973, p. 120).

With such a legacy, small wonder that the sciences still seem to be hostile and unfriendly territory, where a woman's perspective is implicitly suspect and where the woman scientist must do a man's work by imitating a man's viewpoint. Small wonder that Marie Curie confronted hostility from the male scientific establishment even in the twentieth century. Small wonder that for years the scientific contributions of women like Rosalind Franklin (for her work with DNA), Barbara McClintock (genetics), and Lise Meitner (nuclear fission) were overlooked—while some of their male colleagues collected credit and prizes for their efforts in the same projects (Vare and Ptacek, 1988).

A self-fulfilling cycle predominates: scientists value certain characteristics, and they select and encourage "promising" students who have these characteristics. Keller (1985, p. 79) points out that job descriptions of scientists place great value on "autonomy, separation, and distance." In other words, a certain type of personality is idealized as "scientific," and a value system arises that maintains itself by discouraging individuals who don't conform to its standards.

Subjectivity and Objectivity

Prejudice, when it persists, often becomes accepted as fact. One example is the general assumption that women are genetically incapable of logical and impartial reasoning, that women are irrevocably intuitive, "subjective" thinkers while men think rationally, "objectively" (Bardwick, 1971, p. 100).

In contemporary society we still find attitudes that belittle women's lives and work. In 1861 John Stuart Mill discussed the depreciation of women in an essay that is, unfortunately, still appropriate in our time: "I do not know a more signal instance of the blindness with which the world, including the herd of studious men, ignore and pass over all the influences of social circumstances, than their silly depreciation of the intellectual, and silly panegyrics on the moral, nature of women" ([1861] 1986, p. 83).

Much of the argument about women's place in the search for knowledge rests on a distinction between objectivity and subjectivity. The objective (masculine) standard for scientific research embraces Bacon's philosophy of detached observer and domination, which denounces relationship and mutuality as too subjective (feminine).

Knowledge is gained through maintaining a proper distance between the dispassionate observer and the observed, through uniformity and replication of measurement, method, and instruments, and through specification and analysis of results. These techniques seek reliability. The personal view is considered untrustworthy, that is, not replicable. It is too individual, too subjective, and too hard to generalize from. The concept of objectivity requires the scientist to maintain a perspective *outside* of and implicitly *superior* to the phenomenon under observation.

The language of women scientists has been described as a "language of intimacy" (Belenky, Clinchy, Goldberger, and Tarule, 1986, p. 143). Keller (1985) suggests that women researchers may not try to dominate their subjects at all but may feel almost drawn into the phenomena. This different approach has produced impressive results in scientific investigation. It did not lead to false paths but rather to complementary alternatives that supplement the orthodox methodology of scientific research. A scientist's subjective relationship with her material may actually allow her to know it deeply. Subjectivity, when defined and described rigorously, can be an equally valid approach in scientific investigation.

Women continue to be discouraged even after they have completed their training and are at work in the scientific field of their choice. A survey conducted by the Office of Technology Assessment found that women are generally less likely to receive either salary increases or promotions in the scientific professions. In higher education, women scientists are less likely to be appointed to tenure-track positions, to be promoted to tenure, and to achieve full professorships ("Women Scientists Find Barriers in Jobs," 1985).

Such problems are exacerbated for individuals in a two-career marriage. One young couple, Blair and Tom, both research scientists, are wrestling with their need to find a research organization or university that can accommodate them both. They don't compete with each other for the same position since their research is in different fields. But they have to locate a setting where each of them can develop fully into the eminence they both seek, and such a setting is very hard to find. It will require heroic determination from both Blair and Tom to prevent one of them sacrificing a career.

In a world significantly dominated by scientific discovery, by scholars elevated into positions of prominence and influence, by masters of industry and finance, the absence of women in these activities means they are excluded from participating in the arenas and events that inspire and support heroic vision, courage, and inventiveness. Such exclusivity is like tribal prohibitions against sharing sacred information or participating in sacred rite. When women are banned from the arenas in which heroic decisions are made, they are excluded from "a sense of primary heroism" (Becker, 1973, p. 5).

Conclusion

The legends of Prometheus and Eve imply a double standard: knowledge and enterprise are valuable in men but troublesome in women. The conflict between knowledge and innocence began with Eve, and it has been worrisome for women ever since. Women's personal ambition and influence have been distrusted. In the past, women who acknowledged the wish to influence others were seen as witches, enchantresses, or villains. Nowadays they are labeled bossy or bitchy.

Eve is a transitional figure, not only for women but for all humankind. Because she exemplifies an unwillingness to live in credulous innocence and unquestioning obedience, she is called villainous and impudent. She wants to live with her God as a full participant in the world He had created—and into which she was invited.

Innocence outgrown is not villainy. It is a necessary and inevitable step into maturity.

SIX

Necessity Is the Mother of Heroes

Women, I allow, may have different duties to fulfil; but they are human *duties, and the principles that should regulate the discharge of them . . . must be the same.*
—Mary Wollstonecraft, *A Vindication of the Rights of Woman*

Through the ages, women's heroic aspirations and opportunities have depended on the economic and political circumstances of the communities in which they lived. Indeed, the position of the women of any particular society might well be viewed as both a record of its past and a barometer of its present economy.

The common exigencies of life have remained fairly stable over the centuries. People are born, bear children, and die. They must provide food and clothing, find shelter, rear their young, heal the sick and injured, bury their dead, and, whenever possible, establish routines and responsibilities that enable them to live confidently and happily within their communities.

But these ongoing tasks are vulnerable to environmental influences. Heat, rain, drought, famine, abundance, and disease march through prerecorded and recorded time. Other upheavals are man-made: war, migration, territorial conquest, or technological advance. Through all of these, living creatures, plant or animal, have had to adapt in order to survive.

Just as individuals must first cope with emergencies and then try to make sense of them afterward, societies, too, grapple first with urgent needs. Then communal mythologies and religions develop to interpret crises and offer guidelines for their solution in the future. When a heroic myth or ritual outlives its usefulness, it is replaced by a new one, with gods and heroes more appropriate to the community's current needs.

For example, when a society developed to the point where its basic subsistence needs were more or less met through increased skill at cultivation, the community's attention could shift to more complicated mercantile interests. Simple fertility goddesses, who had been worshipped because they represented the promise of adequate nourishment, might be replaced by martial gods and venturesome heroes, whose power and enterprise promoted standards of heroism that could protect accumulated wealth.

What appear to be fixed cultural positions are useful temporary guides, slowly but inevitably subject to revision. But revision comes neither easily nor predictably. Today we see a tension between rapidly changing cultural norms and a traditional base that is reluctant to change. An example is the unwelcome (in some households) public discussion and marketing of condoms and other birth control information on television.

In ancient societies as well as in contemporary ones, an individual's status in the community was based on the nature of her or his contribution to the general welfare and how highly valued that contribution was. Today, the main reason women work is economic; the money women earn is money they and their families need.

In addition to needed income, there is another benefit from working and getting *paid* for it. For women, as for men, pay for work is an acknowledgment that their efforts are important. The wage earner is *recognized* as a valuable member of her society.

When Thelma came to therapy she was at a crossroads. For years she had volunteered in an orphanage as a teacher's aide and had loved her work. But on the rare occasions when she had to miss a day, she didn't like the unspoken sense that, after all, her absence was no big deal; they could pretty easily get along without her. Thelma's children were grown and keeping house for herself and her husband took very little time. Thelma realized that she wanted a job where people considered her work *worthy* and were willing to pay for it. She went back to graduate school, got a school counseling degree, and continues her work with troubled students. She works hard, for little pay. And she loves it. Her paycheck is a receipt from her community attesting that what she does *registers*.

Women and Community

The primitive communities that exist today, while not to be taken as direct templates for the evolution of communities in general, may nevertheless suggest ways subsistence issues affect societal protocol. A look at some contemporary communal systems suggests a possible economic interaction between the prose of everyday life and the poetry of heroic legend.

The delineation of the status of women in five different types of communities (in Africa, Asia, Australia, and the Americas) may serve as a starting point. Martin and Voorhies (1975) describe how women's lives are linked to the simple economic necessities in the following types of communities: (1) foraging, (2) horticultural, (3) pastoralist, (4) agricultural, and (5) industrial. To their list, I would like to add another type, the *mercantile community*, which I put just before the industrial community.

Foraging Communities

In a *foraging* society (the simplest and possibly the earliest social form) community survival is totally dependent upon the successful gathering of whatever resources are available in natural surroundings. Foraging communities have developed their own solutions to the basic problem of what to eat (or whom). Unlike some other animals, who specialize in their food preferences, humans will eat almost anything.

Martin and Voorhies (1975) point out that our clumsy ancestors, not having developed the skill or coordination to make weapons that could guarantee success at hunting, were primarily dependent on whatever vegetation they could forage, relying on it to sustain them between the lucky days when there was meat on the menu. Anthropologists speculate that our early ancestors were grass or seed gatherers who enjoyed a virtual monopoly on this kind of food for two reasons: human manual coordination was superior to the other animals' and human jaws and teeth were well suited for such consumption.

Obviously, such a wilderness home could either be generous, supplying humans with ample food and a comparatively easy existence, or it could be sparse and miserly, imposing a much harsher life. In times of plenty, humans wouldn't have had to compete for food with other animals. They may have enjoyed a relatively trouble-free existence, ranging at will through a provident environment and developing the temperament (and belief system) most congenial with such conditions.

The Garden of Eden may be a nostalgic reminiscence about such a world, with Adam and Eve as the original foragers, gathering what they needed from the trees and the fields around them. Food was dependable in paradise; no talk here of famine or of competition for food with any of the other animals.

Our Biblical ancestors may have constructed an idealized account of an ancient generous milieu and developed a belief system that told of a benign deity. The idyllic community was simple, no in-laws or neighbors, no property rights to defend. What prohibitions there would have been in such a time of plenty would have restricted what one could choose to eat from all the abundance. The greatest danger lay in eating poisonous plants—apples, perhaps?

But this story was told to people who clearly did not live in such a paradise, and they needed an explanation of the disparity with their own laborious existence. It is very likely that many areas did not resemble an idealized paradise. Other areas were not as fertile as the legendary location of the Garden of Eden in the rich alluvial plains between the Tigris and Euphrates rivers (in what is now Iraq). Even this area itself might have been subject to drought and scarcity. Or there could have been an influx of economic refugees from areas where conditions were harsher, thereby increasing the competition for fertile ground and easy harvest. So the story changes to account for hardship.

The Bible was a testament to a new monotheistic faith, but it also had to integrate and supersede legends long taken as truth by people who coexisted with the Hebrews. The Bible had to rework those familiar legends, changing them into new versions and consolidating them within the early Hebrew religion (Friedman, 1987;

Phillips, 1984). The deities of the familiar pagan religions provided the writers of the Bible with examples of easily angered gods who demanded unquestioning obedience and punished offenders severely. The Biblical Jehovah, offended by Adam and Eve's transgressions, expels them from the Garden and destines them to wrest their food from a begrudging soil in the company of animals as likely to be predatory as friendly. Since this same patriarchal turn-of-mind also saw women as either representing failed fertility goddesses or as temptresses, it is not surprising that the expulsion from Eden was explained primarily as Eve's fault (Pagels, 1988).

In contemporary foraging societies, foraging is a female specialty (capitalizing perhaps on women's fine hand/eye coordination). Indeed, Martin and Voorhies (1975) note that women reliably provide more of their tribes' food supply through foraging than is provided through the men's hunting. In such simple tribal economies women are clearly productive contributors.

Such foraging societies are not likely to accumulate surplus or portable wealth. In a generous environment one doesn't think to put something away for a rainy day, and in a harsh one it may not be possible. Since women's toil is as productive as men's and since there is nothing left over to be apportioned, no guardian class of male warriors is necessary, and no effort is devoted to excluding women from access to wealth and power. What wealth there may be is quickly consumed; power is vested in a hierarchy that values agility and perseverance rather than strength and force.

In times of abundance, such societies tend to be egalitarian. Since women are valid economic contributors, they are valued. These societies are often matrilineal and matrilocal: property rights are traced through the maternal line and upon marriage a husband moves into his wife's household. The men are dispersed among relatively stable and peaceable communities.

When the community's surroundings are less favorable and competition for basic necessities becomes a way of life, the role of women changes. Since even a meager diet must be scratched out with great effort from poor soil, the competition for territory becomes intense. Sheer physical strength, which can be used to defend or acquire foraging rights, becomes a valuable asset and overshadows the simple manual dexterity of women.

Under such harsh conditions societies are more likely to be patrilineal and patrilocal. Inheritance of property and foraging rights descends through the male line, and women move in with their husbands. This tradition results in males who assert the rights of their families to specific garden plots and who defend their foraging rights from poachers and trespassers. In such martial heroics, women play no part.

Patrilineal descent is necessarily separatist and exclusive. Sons and brothers must split off from the original family group in order to acquire foraging territory of their own. Economic necessity ruptures family ties and may even foster competition between members of the same family. The classic struggle of brother against brother comes to mind: Cain and Abel, or Joseph and his brothers.

Scarce times also breed modern foragers, as my friend Clare, a teacher in a poverty-stricken section of a big city, discovered. The school provides lunches for its students, and health codes require that food that is not consumed one day must be discarded the next day. Appalled at this waste in the middle of great need, Clare arrives at school very early and secretly sets out the previous day's leftovers on a table in the schoolyard and then goes inside. Long before any of the other teachers arrive, the table is emptied. As if to assert that hunger does not represent poverty of spirit, just before Christmas recess a small paper plate, beautifully decorated with crayon drawings and wrapped in a paper napkin, was left on the table.

Horticultural Communities

The development of horticulture—the deliberate cultivation of the soil and sowing of crops to yield a seasonal and predictable harvest—reflected increased human control over the environment. It represented a more sophisticated understanding of the mechanism of reproduction. Instead of considering fertility a divine function, the early horticulturalists discovered how to use seeds to grow crops. Fertilization was no longer a mysterious and inexplicable phenomenon; though crudely understood, it was relatively controllable.

Partial insight into the mystery of conception brought about a devaluation of women. Unaware of women's contribution to conception, men in these early societies developed a theory that depicted the mother as passive, like the soil in which seed was planted. Woman was only a useful receptacle. This incomplete understanding of reproduction reduced women's contribution to the birth process and made man the central generative character.

Once outside Eden, Eve conceives and gives birth in the distress that is the legacy of her disobedience. To a primitive observer trying to explain the pain involved in childbirth, the simplest explanation (in line with the image of punitive gods) was that the mother's anguish was attributable to divine punishment, once again confirming the inherent wickedness of women. Years ago, one of my friends, a sociologist, told me of a tribe in Africa that held that if the pregnant woman had led a blameless life, the delivery of her child would be painless. I still remember her wry smile as she asked me if I had ever known such a woman or such a delivery.

Yet another development of horticulture affected women's rank in the community. Horticulture, in its most basic form, was more dependent than foraging on a labor-intensive means of production. The necessary brute strength, later supplied by domesticated animals, was first provided by humans. Women were less able, particularly during their childbearing years, to provide a consistent source of the strength and stamina needed to cultivate and irrigate large fields. A woman, although she used the same tool, might not be as productive as a man. The consequent division of labor divided territory into men's workplace (the fields) and women's domain (near the home). Women's efforts were confined to more modest harvests from smaller plots of land, which reduced their economic importance in the community.

Obviously, horticulture allows for increased human control and production of a more dependable food supply. More people can be supported by smaller plots of land. Population becomes denser, and simple social structures develop. Community size is determined by what can be produced in the *leanest* year. Simple coalitions, based on a variety of informal connections, can be formed. Kinship groups develop, as well as voluntary associations based on common need and cooperative effort. Political and religious alliances are formed.

The complex needs of denser populations result in stratification systems wherein the rights and obligations of each person are based on her or his economic contributions. The most productive members of an economy are usually the most dominant politically, and the status system reflects this hierarchical order. Since men were responsible for the most ample production of food and surplus, they became more esteemed than women. Their economic contributions were more prestigious, and their virtues and privileges were eventually explained as divinely ordained.

Along with the increasing dominance of men in horticultural societies, patrilocality becomes more common; the wife is likely to move to her husband's residence and live out the rest of her life there, possibly in the company of other women of the same household. The Biblical story of Ruth and Naomi, for example, is a story that extols patrilocality: Ruth goes to live in her husband's community and chooses to remain there with her mother-in-law even after his death.

Contemporary patrilocal tribes offer some interesting insights. If the new wife is a foreigner, she is believed to be fickle, treasonous, and "surreptitiously destructive." In these primitive societies, transplanted women are considered worthless, fit only for menial supportive activities. They are to be mute and passive participants in community activities. The exceptional vocal or assertive woman is "both resented and feared by men. Indeed [she is] viewed as a reflection of the ultimate depravity of womankind" (Martin and Voorhies, 1975, p. 266).

But, as we have seen, speech develops early in women, and women's protests are more likely to be verbal rather than physical. Societal restrictions against articulate opposition are ways of silencing criticism or dissent in troubled times. Speaking out then becomes a heroic activity.

The Bible, reflecting its many authors and the long period of its development, is inconsistent. In some sections it inveighs against outspokenness in women and directs women to remain with their families, modest, solicitous, and dependent. But the Bible also has several examples of articulate and forthright women who deserve respect: Sarah, who converses familiarly with God; Miriam, who guards her baby brother as he floats in the bulrushes and whose prophecy and singing inspired Moses and the Israelites in their journey through the desert; and Deborah, who presided in judgment as she sat under a palm tree.

We, too, are inconsistent in our reaction to outspoken women. Margaret O'Toole had to wait five years for vindication of her charge that her superior in molecular biology research had actually invented some data. Finally supported by an investigation of the National Institutes of Health, she is still bitter about the accusations of mental instability and the fact that she was without work in scientific research for four years. She had to take a job answering phones at her brother's moving company (Weiss, 1991; Hilts, 1991).

Pastoralist Communities

Pastoralist communities, organized around the intensive herding or use of animals, may have originated as spin-offs of early agricultural communities. Effective exploitation of a familiar environment, resulting in adequate food and characterized by little competition, seems to promote a matrilineal adaptation. In sedentary pastoral societies, therefore, where pastures are close to the permanent settlements, women may be involved in some form of cultivation and can achieve some communal respect for their economic contributions.

But nomadic and seminomadic societies may not stay long enough in any one place to sow or harvest any but the most minimal crops. The simple foraging or light horticultural contribution of women becomes less important to the tribal economy, and is reflected in women's diminished status.

The more mobility characterizing the pastoralist way of life, the more subordinate is the position of women. When the males of the tribe separate from the women to wander along with their flocks and return home only periodically, it becomes important to control women's behavior during men's absence. Women's participation and status in the community are ritually restricted.

Not surprisingly, the customs of the tribe, such as the segregation of women and the protocols about the care of the flocks, may be provided sacred rationalizations. Women's subordinacy could be ensured through ritual and myths that enforce a repressive and limiting code. Women's clothing and conduct could thus be inflexibly defined, with severe punishments for even small deviations. The chador, the almost total cover-up dress of Islamic women, is an example of such regulation.

There are parallels in American history. In the 1700s, Amerindian men tamed the horses descended from those brought over by the Spanish explorers. The consequent increased mobility and range of the Indian braves enhanced their hunting, provided an abundant supply of meat and tradable furs, and made them wealthy. At the same time, however, the "social and economic revolution brought about by the use of horses" reduced the once considerable power of the women of those tribes. "The romance and daring of war and hunting dominated the ritual life of the group" (Evans, 1989, p. 16). In the warlike rituals that became more frequent, women were assigned one role: spectator.

The participation of Indian women in the economic and political governance of their tribes was vigorously undermined by European settlers. The settlers brought with them beliefs that recommended submissive and dependent behavior for women. Missionaries, horrified by the energy and assertion of these sturdy Amerindian women, were quick to teach them the "proper" values.

Early American pastoralist customs were predominately patriarchal and patrilocal, as exemplifed by the ethos of the American explorer, rancher, or cowboy. In this tradition, women were to remain in the towns, restricted to roles as casual sexual entertainment or protected wives.

But the spirit of these women in conjunction with the risky settling of the American West and Midwest created conflicts. Early settlements, where women were scarce and crucially important for survival, demanded an egalitarian practicality that contradicted the patriarchal territorialism of cattlemen.

Nevertheless, even though they were useful and resourceful, women were equal only if economic necessity demanded it, as in early American colonial times or in the homesteading era. But even in colonial America there were certain crafts, such as "working in wood and leather and metal" that were traditionally closed to women (Cowan, 1983).

Even today, the nomadic way of life is primarily a man's option. Although mobility is becoming a way of life for many women, the pull is still greater for women to attend to their children and their families. While they are not tribally restricted to home territory, many women describe the conflict between a career of their own and the call of home.

My patient Beth lost her husband in an accident and reared their two young sons alone. She did this with devotion, energy, humor, and directness. When the boys were young, she decided it was important to provide them with a stable life by establishing a home where they could feel secure and bring their friends. So, like the women of the early settlements who remained home while their husbands blazed trails through uncharted wilderness, Beth's priority was roots. Now, twenty-one years later, she is moving into a new phase in her life. Her sons are "launched," and she is ready to launch herself. There are places in the world she wants to see, friends in distant lands she wants to be with again, and people she doesn't yet know to meet.

Often the wife who leads a nomadic existence (in order to accommodate her husband's career, for example) seems to encounter special difficulties. There are two ways she is affected. As the wife of a mobile worker, she is the one who supervises the frequent moves from one community to another. Over and over again, she establishes a home, enters and supports their children in one new school after another, and builds the social connections that make the new community feel like home.

As the mobile professional herself, she may be even more isolated. She either moves from one community to another or remains based in one location and travels frequently. Either way, her personal life suffers.

In a group therapy session, Shelley, a very successful labor arbitrator, reported that she traveled around the country more often than she stayed home. One night she dreamed she was remodeling a house she lived in and that she was very dissatisfied with the way it turned out. One large pillar kept getting in the way, right in the middle of the parlor. I asked Shelley to imagine that she was the house and to describe what was wrong with her. She surprised herself by saying, "There isn't enough living room in me!" When she heard this, she nodded and resolved to "remodel her own living room" by spending more time at home and keeping connected to the people she loved.

Agricultural Communities

A major technological breakthrough opened the way for the development of the agricultural society. The simple digging stick, the
basic implement of the horticultural community, was dramatically
improved, which ushered in a new era in the continual struggle for
subsistence. Adding a pair of handles and hitching the new contrap-
tion to an ox created the plow. It became the "instrument of surplus" (Burke, 1978, p. 9). Urban civilization, with its complex
network of human interactions, was born.

The production and protection of surplus generate certain
consequences. Small plots of land can provide for a larger number
of people, and the possibility of surplus arises. Surplus can be marketed, which increases the complexity of transactions and exchanges. The accumulation of wealth becomes possible. A wealthy
community needs police and armies to defend its wealth from pred-
ators both from within and outside of its borders. It needs legislators
and regulators to adjudicate the terms of commerce. Furthermore,
efficient transportation and communication channels are necessary
to maintain the coherence and efficiency of the increasingly complex community. Truly urban settlements, based on increased productivity, emerged as the most efficient setting for the exchange of
goods and services.

Agriculture, based on the control of domesticated and powerful animal labor, required a powerful hand on the plow. Even
more important, it enabled a single person to plow still larger and
larger fields. Banding together for defense of land-based wealth became very important in sedentary farming communities, so a warrior class developed. Warriors, richly rewarded by the spoils of their
victories, soon became more important than farmers.

The production of surplus had an enormous effect on the
status of women. An even greater cultural differentiation of the
sexes evolved that governed women's social, sexual, and working
behaviors. For women, the demands associated with bearing and
rearing children became even more restrictive; women were even
more isolated within or near the house and began to solely perform
those duties necessary for the maintenance of the family. They were
no longer important producers of food or of any marketable sur-

plus. Female labor became restricted to the domestic setting, and women's status and influence outside the home declined further. The mythology to support this stratification was true-to-form; women's subordinacy was either rationalized as innate or idealized as divinely ordained.

Mercantile Communities

Early cities began as informal bartering centers and then developed into centers for the communication of essential information, locations for religious observance, and sites where important economic and political decisions were reached (Burke, 1978). Economics was key to the operation of the city, and the most influence was exerted by the most productive citizens.

Craftsmen, makers of tools and weapons, workers in metal, leather, and stone, designers and builders of the complicated structures needed to accommodate the increasing density of population and manufacture—all of these people traded their wares and skills for the food and other necessities that they did not produce for themselves. In some workshops, slave labor, both adult and child, was the basis for productivity.

Accumulation of wealth depended on the development of such institutions as slavery, commerce, trade, warfare, property, and inheritance rights. The accumulation of wealth also continued the functional stratification of the citizenry into those who exercised influence and those who did not. The Greek polis was such a community. By employing the enforced labor of slaves, the social system freed its more fortunate citizens for elevated pursuits such as philosophical debates, aesthetic studies, and athletic contests.

Women were irrelevant except as supportive or decorative background figures. Devoted wives and mothers were disqualified from full citizenship and equal status because they were only of limited value in civilizations increasingly dependent on force. Wives or slaves, their economic contributions were carefully defined. The heroism of women was subordinated to the ambitions of the society.

Urban heroes served the needs of a mercantile, preindustrial society interested in the latest technological advances, the possession of negotiable wealth, and exclusive access to world markets and trade routes. In this regard, the legendary adventures of the Greek heroes are open to provocative reinterpretations.

Jason, for example, who with his intrepid band of Argonauts sailed the Mediterranean in quest of the Golden Fleece, demonstrated more than his courage and his right to rule Iolcus. He was also asserting his right and the right of his crew—symbolically composed of representative heroes from neighboring cities—to traffic in the trade routes of the time. Not unlike the struggle of sixteenth-century England against an armada that locked it into a tiny island economy, Jason's aim was to expand territorial claims to include unchallenged access to any port in the Mediterranean.

Even Jason's quest of the Golden Fleeece may have had a mercantile purpose contained within a gleaming metaphor. Sheepskins were once used in the smelting of gold. Gold particles were washed and filtered through a sheepskin, which was then hung on a branch to dry—even as the Golden Fleece—and then burned, destroying the skin and leaving little blobs of gold in the ashes (Burke, 1978).

So Jason's heroism may have served at least two purposes: establishing passage rights through contested waterways and learning a new technology for processing a precious commodity. Both of these enterprises are still practiced effectively today by our modern mercantile heroes, though perhaps not with such dash or publicity. The astronauts of our day, who navigate the contested oceans of outer space in the service of espionage and commercial advantage, are direct descendants of Jason.

Assertive, aggressive, shrewd, powerful, venturesome, competitive—these were the heroic qualities that appealed to communities then and are familiar to us even now. These were masculine virtues. This was the period of empire building, of aggrandizement, and of defense and offense. These activities required an elaborate and dependable support system. Religion, legends, and tellers of hero tales all obliged in this transitional time.

Industrial Communities

In our modern industrial society we perceive a blending of these other societies. Our modern foragers are the urban homeless; agribusiness has taken over the family farm, where there was at least the possibility of some economic cooperation between husband and wife; organization executives (still predominantly men) have become our modern nomads. In some instances the husband's success includes a wife who either stays home while he makes his career or travels with him to his new job—a modern patrilocal arrangement. Our modern pastoralists now shepherd stocks, bonds, and takeovers.

And the people who regulate all this activity are predominantly men.

One of the most contradictory and fascinating aspects of the development of the industrial society in the United States is the initial centrality and eventual displacement of women. In the early 1800s men were still engaged in farming and were therefore unavailable to work in the developing textile industry. So women (and sometimes children) operated the machines. A young woman who might have been an economic burden to her family could become a wage earner.

True to the customs of the day, the model factory towns in New England were still patriarchal; communal living arrangements for the young women were carefully regulated, and the women could be shuttled from factory to farm as needed (Lerner, 1979).

The values of an industrial society support a patriarchal ethos. Apply some of these dynamics in our present world. When times are hard, women must work. But men's status has traditionally been based on their economic superiority and self-sufficiency, so men who fear loss of status because of women working will need some reassurance. A social etiquette will be developed to counteract the loss of male self-esteem.

Such protocols may, for one thing, ensure lower pay for women. Hewlett (1986, p. 74) describes how economists explain it: "Those on the liberal left . . . emphasize the fact that women are paid less because they are discriminated against; those on the conservative right stress that home and family responsibilities depress their earnings potential."

But wage inequity has tragic consequences. Many single women find that their earnings are inadequate to meet their needs. If the woman is the head of a household and has responsibility for children or aged parents, her salary is rarely sufficient. She lives on the brink of poverty, if not actually in it. If she is living alone, there is, in addition, the constant worry about coping with catastrophic surprises.

Another disturbing fact is that the jobs and professions staffed mainly by women (nursing, elementary school teaching, and so on) are not only underpaid but vaguely disrespected. For example, one woman described how a friend introduced her as "almost a doctor." Actually, she is a nurse and proud of her profession. She protests, "Feminism will have succeeded not only when women have access to all fields but when traditionally female professions like nursing gain the high value and solid social respect they deserve" (Baer, 1991, p. 24).

In reaction to the poverty that many women endure, they have developed a practical heroism. They trade services with each other and form cooperatives that reduce the cost of food and other necessities. Indeed, I have even heard of an informal bartering or borrowing system. One family, for example, might trade the use of a sofa bed for the loan of another family's appliance for a specified period of time.

A strong fundamentalist backlash opposes the mobility and public prominence of women. Women are admonished to exchange independence for male protection against a dangerous and seductive world. The implication is that women, like Eve, are unable to protect themselves against evil influence or to resist temptation and need a strong male helpmate to take care of them. These fundamentalists have evidently forgotten Adam's sturdy example.

Several years ago I received a phone call in response to a letter I had written to the editor of our local newspaper. I had protested against the censorship of a sensitively filmed, sexually explicit movie (mild by present-day standards). A male caller asked if I didn't fear men who would have seen the movie and then gone on to rape innocent women. In order to make his point, he asked if I had seen a number of movies that he considered incitant. It turned out that he had seen them all; I hadn't seen any.

Despite the fact that women contribute their own paychecks to the family economy and they now have the right to vote (which suggests that their opinions are being voiced and attended to), it is commonly recognized that women are still drastically underrepresented among executives, administrators, governors, congressional representatives, judges and, other arbiters of influence and decision. There are still questions about women's ability to make tough judgments and to be objective. When Representative Patricia Schroeder was weighing whether to run for the presidency, she was asked whether she would campaign as a woman. She answered, "I never knew I had an option" (Nadelson, 1990, p. 512). Fickle, emotional, and untrustworthy, women are deemed unfit for high office and ineligible for heroic decision making. The reliance on women for supportive participation must certainly suggest to thoughtful people that those supportive services require the same qualities. But somehow this inconsistency persists.

Conclusion

Economic and political circumstances are powerful determinants of the status of women at any given time and in any given community. These circumstances dictate whether women are recognized as equals and participate fully in their community or relegated to minor and supportive roles. In either case, sacred or secular myths will offer justifications for the position of women in that particular society. These myths will define how women are supposed to behave and how their behavior will be interpreted.

SEVEN

The Geography
of Heroism

*A woman should be good for everything at home, but
abroad good for nothing.*
—Euripides, *Meleager*

The geography of heroic action was for many years either unexplored "virgin" lands or territory controlled by hostile forces that were to be overcome and conquered. Centuries ago, in a world where so much terrain remained unknown, discovery and exploration were seen as the work of heroes. And then, since most of the newly discovered countries were already inhabited, domination and conquest soon followed, all male activities, all generously chronicled by historians and cartographers. The victors, as they usually do, designated the scenes of heroic behavior and also named its leading players—themselves. Historians subsequently acquiesced.

Women, less likely to be the explorers to find the virginal territories or the warriors to subdue them, have been the heroes who come to know and love the land and make it habitable for others yet to come, for example, the homesteading wife or the pioneer-of-the-prairies heroine in Willa Cather's *My Antonia* (1977). Nevertheless, in the simple statistics of history, since women were not the "first" into unclaimed territory, their heroism was not recorded.

The historians who chronicled the world's heroic events were interested mainly in the "transmission and exercise of power" (Lerner, 1979, p. 3). An adequate acknowledgment of the heroism of the women requires that historians look in "obscure" and different places. Furthermore, when they find the story of a woman there, they must adopt a different standard of heroism, one that may not reckon influence in terms of square miles of territory captured.

It's a little like the joke about the drunk who loses his keys in a dark part of the street but who insists on looking for them under the street lamp because the light is better there. Historians have simply continued a long-established pattern. The "right" theater of action is the masculine one highlighted in the Bible and in Greek and Roman legends. The less dramatic deeds of women and other "powerless" individuals were simply not included in legends, religious tradition, or history because they didn't take place on the lighted stage.

Heroic Terrain

A grim geography set the scene for one prospector's wife, stranded in a summer cabin in Alaska. An avalanche had injured her and isolated her from other people, including her husband. She faced a harsh Alaskan winter alone—and pregnant. She improvised splints for her broken arm and leg, burned the wooden floor of the cabin piece by piece for warmth, and unraveled the flour sack to make string to tie the umbilical cord of the baby she was expecting, knowing she would have to deliver it herself. Incredibly, both Martha Martin and her baby survived. She kept a diary that winter, "to keep my sanity" (Moffat and Painter, 1975, p. 301).

Alaska in the early 1950s was still primarily man's territory, and Martha was there simply as her husband's companion. Traditional legend would have depicted her assisting him or falling into some predicament that would call forth heroic effort from him. His adventures would be the central heroic theme. Her own independent survival would be neither the expected subject nor the classic pattern of a hero tale. But listen to her account of that winter.

Pregnant, Martha describes killing a one hundred pound otter and laboriously dragging him home and skinning him. After eating the heart and the liver, she sets about to make a robe for her baby out of the otter's hide. "My darling child may be born in a lowly cabin, but she shall be wrapped in one of the earth's most costly furs" (p. 302).

As the winter wears on, Martha observes the animals and birds who visit the cabin and comes to know their postures and moods. She sets out boughs and the remains of the otter to feed them. And finally, when she baptizes her newborn daughter, she bakes bread to distribute to her neighbors, the deer, as a "christening feast."

Her diary is filled with the details of daily life: how she softened the otter skin, how she cut her hair down to the scalp to prevent the mice from nibbling at the head wounds she had treated with bacon grease, and how she set a bouquet of cedar and hemlock at her window to give it "a nice look, as though a man and a woman lived here."

In the spring, when friendly Indians finally return to their fishing camp nearby, she cleans the cabin, puts flowers at the window, makes coffee, and dresses her daughter in her best clothes. When the time comes to go back with the Indians to the settlement, Martha says wistfully that she almost didn't want to leave at all. She doesn't say why.

Perhaps she had learned about the heroic in herself, and she sensed that returning to her customary life would either contradict or nullify that knowledge. She had learned by herself to ensure her survival and the survival of the baby who depended on her. She had mastered the trials of winter and had come to feel equal to—even partnered by—those wintry conditions rather than intimidated by them. Her current challenge was to find a way to fit such spirit back into the familiar geography.

Martha's diary celebrates the indomitability of her spirit and her assertion of human dignity, even when there is no other person to acknowledge them. As we read her entries we are struck by the fact that although her heroism contains many of the basic qualities of heroism (stamina, ingenuity, persistence, and physical and mental courage), she also masters her isolation in ways that seem essentially womanly.

What is womanly about her heroism is its affinity to the setting where it occurred. For her, geography was neither a stage for a grand adventure nor an adversary to be conquered: it was a pervasive *context* for interactions with her surroundings. In everything she does we can feel a strong sense of another presence—either her unborn baby or the birds, the deer or the hoped-for Indians—to whom she relates in the midst of her isolation. The personal well from which she draws her heroic strength is her sense of response to challenge in relationship *to*, not as victory *over*.

Today, for many contemporary women, heroic geography is experienced in terms of relationship. Martha was reluctant to leave her Alaskan cabin because she had discovered something essential about herself there. Helen, on the other hand, chose to leave the familiar geography of a lifetime in order to find herself. In her fifties, divorced from her husband of many years whom she had married right out of high school, Helen left the city in which she had lived all her life and spent ten years supporting herself and living as a single woman in a new city. She could have remained comfortably established in her hometown, but she sensed she needed to strike out into new territory. She began with a mix of feelings: fright and excitement in equal measure. But slowly the balance changed. Now in her sixties, about to marry again, Helen says that after living alone for ten years she really knows how to be married.

Debra, a social worker, explains her volunteer home-visit work with nonhospitalized AIDS patients with a shrug of her shoulders. "There is so much they need, some of them are so afraid of death. I felt it was the least I could do." These are people who are so traumatized by their disease that they would never sit in an agency waiting room. The stigma some of them feel makes them voluntarily limit their geography. So Debra enters their territory by going to their homes, encouraging them to seek medical help, teaching their friends how best to comfort them, and helping them confront death with dignity and presence.

Children waiting in the corridors of courthouses during divorce and custody hearings often feel lonely and frightened. Selma, a delicate, grandmotherly woman, entered these corridors. After taking a training program to prepare her, she is now regularly assigned to sit with, listen to, and otherwise take care of the children who are left alone and unattended. They can talk to her about their feelings. She says it is the most exciting thing she has done.

Women's Heroic Terrain: The Pedestal

Throughout history, women have been given easy access to one particular piece of turf—the pedestal. Idealized female figures have

long graced public pedestals and monuments like the Statue of
Liberty, blindfolded figures of Justice, and noble icons of other
virtues. They appear as heroic and inspiring figures in parks and
at historic battlefields, in murals on the inner walls of public buildings and in bas-reliefs on the exteriors. There they stand, frozen into
time-honored poses of nobility and inspiration, summoning men to
deeds of daring and promising them glory.

Once again women are reduced to idealized but static images:
archetypal figures of inspiration, prizes to be heroically pursued,
individuals protected and won by men. Many of the pedestal figures
stand with laurel wreath in hand, perpetually ready to congratulate
and reward the hero who will do battle for them. Immobilized themselves, they call for active champions and promise them rewards for
their efforts.

Unlike male statues, which are more likely to depict actual
historical figures (generals, statesmen, authors), most female figures
aren't identifiable as individuals (Warner, 1985). These marble and
bronze images merely continue the ancient tradition of submerging
the individual identity of women in the service of communal mythology. As Martha Banta (1987, p. 9) says, "More often than not,
the types that stood for national values were female in form."

Think a moment, though, how incongruous it is to have a
female figure of justice when real women are so clearly underrepresented on the bench. Anonymous figures of women mock the fact
that their presence in heroic places has been decided not by women
but by men with the authority to commission public monuments.
So we have the irony of women, real or symbolic, invited into public
places to commemorate heroic events in which actual women were
allowed little participation. Whether as memorial statues or live
women breaking bottles of champagne on the hulls of ships, wom-
en's forays into heroic locales are limited to graceful gestures;
women are mere decorative accessories to the celebration of the more
substantial accomplishments of influential men.

Men's Heroic Terrain: Women's Limited Access

Even now, when qualified women are increasingly numerous, there
are many settings where women's presence is more the exception

than the rule. Women have limited access, for example, to prominent positions in government council chambers, to laboratories, to seats of judgment and negotiation, to construction sites, and to the controls of mighty equipment. Although these settings are certainly not the only places where heroism occurs, the heroism that takes place there commands attention. These places are both public and publicized.

In the geography of work, a woman in an airplane seems just fine in the role of flight attendant cheerfully doling out coffee, but her fitness behind the controls of that same aircraft takes longer to accept. A woman in the halls of Congress as secretary to a male senator poses no problems, but voters (and this sadly includes women) have proved remarkably reluctant to send her there as a senator herself.

The majority of women who *are* elected to Congress are in the House of Representatives, *not* the Senate, which is often referred to as the "upper" house (Baxter and Lansing, 1983.) Women's underrepresentation was dramatized in the recent hearings for the confirmation of Judge Clarence Thomas's appointment to the Supreme Court. Not one woman was sitting on the Judiciary Committee, although the lives of millions of women would be affected by Thomas's decisions as a Supreme Court Justice and despite the fact that one of the most crucial statements was the testimony of a woman, Professor Anita Hill, alleging sexual harassment by Judge Thomas.

Women are achieving some success in *local* politics. They are being elected mayors in increasing numbers, more women are being appointed to state cabinet-level positions, and the number of women in state legislatures has quadrupled since 1969 ("Women Gain in State Posts," 1988). However, their entry into national office is slow; at the present rate of 5.4 percent increase every seventy years, equality of representation in Congress will not arrive until the year 2582! (Nye, 1990).

It is tempting to speculate that a mayor may appear to voters like a municipal housekeeper, a glorified domestic expert who sees to it that the trash is picked up and the streets are swept, and so women are seen as eligible. What they are doing, in the terms of an early women's reform movement, has actually been called "social housekeeping" (Anderson and Zinsser, 1988b, p. 398).

But the next hurdles are much higher. The mayor of Princeton, Barbara Boggs Sigmund, who was considering running for governor of New Jersey, believes escalation is risky. The danger, she said, is that "you become perceived as personally ambitious rather than a high-minded, dedicated public servant. You're caught in the bind of your femininity" (Foderaro, 1989, p. 29). Note the use of the term *servant*. Even so, in 1990 there were women running for governor in several states.

The participation of women, some 30,000 of them, in the war in the Persian Gulf further legitimized the entry of women into another region of male geography. Women piloted supply planes into combat, they served as aircraft maintenance technicians, they directed anti-Scud missiles. They were injured, they lost their lives, they were captured; in short, they were comrades-at-arms.

These women had both public and unpublicized predecessors. In World War II, Great Britain registered all women between the ages of eighteen and fifty and conscripted single women between the ages of twenty and thirty. The conscripted women were given a choice between military service or work in factories or on farms (Anderson and Zinsser, 1988b). In World War II, scores of women ferried war planes from one base to another in the United States and from aircraft factories in England to the RAF bases in British and European battle zones. Women pilots ran counter to society's expectations, and as a result, this activity remained little known.

Diana Barnato Walker was one of the many women who served in the Air Transport Auxiliary during World War II ferrying fighter planes from factories to locations around Britain in preparation for a dreaded Nazi invasion. She describes the terror of flying without radio contact, sometimes because the planes were so new they didn't have radios and sometimes to avoid interference with "the very busy channels of the RAF communications" (Saywell, 1985, p. 9).

Little was made public about the hundreds of British women—like Joan Savage Cowey, a member of the women's Auxiliary Territorial Service—who drove trucks and transports between army bases and operated searchlights at antiaircraft stations. Other women were airlifted into occupied France and Poland, where they worked as spies, demolition agents, and organizers of underground routes for escaping prisoners.

Since they were female, these women could not officially be considered combatants, even though many of them flew into contested airspace and risked their lives daily in other operations. British women who served in scenes of combat were required to sign the Official Secrets Act, which meant that their participation under fire had to be kept secret. The result of this was that even after the war, these women remained officially unacknowledged. One of them later observed, "You could say the forgotten army was not the one in Burma, but the one in skirts" (Saywell, 1985, p. 9).

In the United States a new model for women emerged: Rosie the Riveter. She inspired women to fill the factories making weapons and equipment. Posters appeared, with her smiling radiantly, wearing protective goggles and gloves, her hair neatly covered by a kerchief. But this was a temporary image. As soon as the war was over, Rosie disappeared. Women were released to go back to their proper place—home—and to free up the jobs for returning veterans, who would make the refrigerators and automobiles that disappeared during the war.

During World War II in occupied Poland, France, and Italy, hundreds of women saw their countries, their villages, and their very neighborhoods become combat zones, where a familiar metro station could become the setting for entrapment and betrayal and an ordinary streetcar could be the scene for search and interrogation by armed enemy soldiers. In these suddenly alien settings, women served heroically, staffing underground armies of resistance, ambushing enemy troops, transporting arms in innocent-looking baskets or under their coats, and carrying messages throughout a secret network.

Women memorized phone numbers and addresses and "forgot" them just as quickly, and in scenes of secret torture they did not betray their comrades: "Again their stupid questions. They are hitting me. Blows fall about my head and over my body. They aim for my wound. I refuse to cry out. I won't give them the satisfaction. They hit my breasts often during the interrogations. They break my teeth, my jaw. My gums bleed, my teeth crack. I say nothing" (Saywell, 1985, p. 59). No medal for this small Frenchwoman, Brigitte

Friang. Only unspeakable years in a Nazi concentration camp, a life haunted by nightmares—and an indelible firsthand knowledge of the brutality that humans are capable of.

In Holland, Miep Gies risked her life daily to bring food and news of the outside to the family and friends of Anne Frank, hidden in the attic from the Nazis. She kept them alive for years until their eventual discovery and imprisonment.

Currently, Jemera Rone covers Central and South America for a human rights organization. Her job is to get firsthand information through on-the-spot interviews with soldiers and refugees; her heroism invades jungles and back roads, and her weapons are tapes, notebooks, and cameras ("Heroes for Hard Times," 1988).

Betty Miller, a nice gray-haired woman, lived in an inner-city subsidized housing project so tough that she bought a pistol to defend herself. As she came to know her neighbors, she discovered that many of them didn't know how to read. She set about teaching them. But she was no benevolent lady of good works; when her pupils got troublesome she said to them, "Sit down and shut up and I'll teach ya to read." Betty now wants to extend her teaching to individuals in the prison system, convinced that a program teaching reading would reduce the number of repeaters (Huff, 1988).

History, Sports, and Heroic Geography

Throughout history, the athletic field has rivaled the battlefield as a scene of male heroics. Both the Trojan War and the battles of Alexander the Great were interrupted on ceremonial occasions so that the warriors could participate in funerary athletic games (Keegan, 1987). The early Greek Olympics were exclusively male contests.

As it was for the ancient Greeks, heroism on the playing field today is equated almost exclusively with men's efforts. It's no news that the greatest attention and financial support, both in school gyms and in professional settings, go to men's sports. The rush and excitement of competition, of defeat and victory, are predominantly male. The big leagues, the ones with the high salaries, and adulation of sports heroes are all dominated by male athletes. Young boys collect baseball cards and T-shirts with the numbers of their football heroes, favorite basketball players, and soccer idols.

Girls' and women's team sports, on the other hand, are chronically underfunded and virtually ignored. Our sense of the proper geography for women accepts them easily on the tennis courts and golf courses. But even there they don't get the same attention. The greatest harvest of publicity for a marvelous woman tennis player, Billie Jean King, came after she competed against an over-the-hill male tennis player, Bobby Riggs. Until then her contests—against other women—had received little notice. When a man stepped onto the court the competition became worthy of note.

This tennis match is seen by some as the beginning of a new era. Women's tennis, golf, and track competitions are now getting national television coverage. The women who participate in the Olympic Games have had a powerful impact on the heroic aspirations of ambitious young women. Powerful, dedicated athletes like Chris Evert, Martina Navratilova, and Florence Kersee-Joyner are redefining women's place in sports. It is not mere coincidence that recently a young girl was allowed to play placekicker on a boys' football team.

Betty is a teenager who takes ballet lessons and loves them. To improve her stamina, she also participates in a physical fitness training program where her fellow students are all boys. She says that the programs for girls were just not challenging enough. But it is not easy to be the only girl; she takes a lot of ribbing. Not unlike the hazing that some women get when they invade a traditional male workplace (Josefowitz and Gadon, 1988).

It is certainly an unlikely brotherhood, but modern historians and sports writers (each in their own way) resemble the mythmakers who preceded them. Greek and Roman hero tales long ago established the preeminence of stories about power, competition, and physical mastery. Sports writers, like historians, deal with the statistics of the playing fields: "facts" in terms of champions, victories, and defeats.

By the time human tribes were sophisticated enough to record their beliefs in written form (the Hebrews in the Bible and the Greeks in the epic tales of Homer and the instructive poetry of Hesiod), communities had already developed into complex organi-

zations with clear stipulations for appropriate male and female behavior. Ritual and law defined who had access to certain public
forums and business places. These geographical prohibitions
merely confirmed and sanctified the pattern that already existed.
Sexual geography, dictating where women were allowed to go and
how they were to behave there, was elevated above ordinary human
decision making and declared divine law.

The Bible instructed men and women about how to live,
about the proper behavior and proper settings for each sex. A
"woman of valor" was one who "worketh willingly with her hands
. . . giveth food to her household . . . reacheth forth her hands to
the needy . . . girdeth her loins and maketh strong her arms" (Prov.
31). When she does this, she is clothed in "strength and dignity."

Her husband meanwhile is "known in the gates, when he
sitteth with the elders of the land" (Prov. 31). But when a *woman*
appears in public places, she is "riotous and rebellious. Her feet
abide not in her house; Now she is in the streets, now in the broad
places" (Prov. 7). She is disreputable, a harlot, unfaithful to her
husband (who is, remember, not at home), and she is to be shunned.

In the Bible, women were instructed not to seek influence in
public or religious affairs and not to seek public attention for their
accomplishments. A clear distinction was made between the private
world, where women had much to do, and the public world, where
they had no place. Women's authority was to be personal and domestic, rooted in family geography, and effective only within a
circle of intimates. Women's valor was a private trait, known only
to family. When a woman is known, it is because her husband and
family speak of her; her works are known publicly, but there is no
statement that she herself should appear there. "Her children rise
up and call her blessed; her husband also" (Prov. 31).

Women authors of the early gothic adventure novels in
nineteenth-century Europe continued the cloistered tradition. Although these authors sent their heroines into strange exotic lands,
their adventures there still occurred *inside* large castles or mansions
(Moers, 1976).

Even great writers, many of whom were extraordinary by contemporary standards, were surprisingly traditional in their treatment
of heroines. "Nominally ceded the private sphere, women are sup-

posed to leave the public realm untouched" (Edwards, 1984). Within enclosed spaces these heroines wandered, entered deserted rooms, and found strange prisoners, pale invalids, or assaultive lunatics behind locked doors, in musty, unused wings of great houses.

But there were subtle signs of protest in some of these novels. Cathy in Emily Brontë's *Wuthering Heights* epitomizes women's dilemma. She chooses to make a life for herself indoors, in the parlors of genteel society, but to do so she must renounce her birthright to wander on the untamed moors. Because Cathy denies her own wild primitivism, Brontë suggests, she dooms herself to become a lost soul trying, even after death, to return to her true lover and her true home. Cathy represents women's struggle against the geography of their "proper" place—at home and within four walls.

Women novelists like the Brontës understood this alienation (unconsciously, perhaps) and often invented a woman villain symbolically the evil double of the virtuous but unhappy heroine. Such a character represents the part of her nature that the heroine must disown in order to conform to the permissible stereotypes. Charlotte Brontë's proud heroine, Jane Eyre, found her nemesis in the attic of the mansion where she was governess. Although possessing a strong spirit, outwardly Jane was contained and well-behaved. But in the attic lived a lunatic woman who was not at all willing to be confined and whose fiery rage brought down the whole household (Gilbert and Gubar, 1979).

The sad fact is that most popular novels of the eighteenth and nineteenth centuries did not encourage women to think deeply beyond the domestic and the familiar. The novel's geography had little breadth, and what breadth it had was measured in vertical concerns about status. Jane Austen's lively (but eminently respectable) heroines plot and gossip in drawing rooms and dream only of good marriages and large mansions with large manicured gardens in careful enclosures. This was what women could hope for, and Austen keenly described the wit and intelligence that women used (and concealed) to achieve such vicarious successes.

Fallen or exceptional women whose lives were exciting but doomed lived outside the conventions, and their "outsidedness" was frequently defined geographically. Madame Bovary leaves her provincial backwater town in a frantic and pitiful search for liveliness and excitement. Camille's noble renunciation of her lover for his family's welfare doesn't compensate for her status as a *demimondaine*, a creature of questionable reputation who lives in a disreputable "half-world." Poor Scarlett O'Hara (who was a twentieth-century heroine even though *Gone with the Wind* was set in the nineteenth) was no more shrewd and conniving than Rhett Butler. But after leaving her genteel way of life (actually she was dispossessed), she comes to a lonely and disppointed end. And at the end, all she wants to do is go home to Tara. She has learned her lesson and accepts fit punishment for venturing successfully into the unladylike terrain of commerce and, even worse, besting men at their own game.

It's not sufficient to say that these fictions reflected the actual lives and experiences of women. In novels of this same period, men were exploring utopias of various descriptions, surviving on desert islands, journeying to exotic countries, and voyaging into space and under oceans. Men's horizons were not restricted to the familiar skylines of everyday life.

When so many women today must work either to support themselves or to supplement their partner's inadequate income, they find themselves in what has been called the "pink collar ghetto." But some women are indomitable; because of the low pay for women's work, many women are trying to get apprenticed into jobs as carpenters, plumbers, and construction workers where the pay scale is higher.

Heroic Geography Today

The belief that a woman's sphere of activity should be restricted to her own home or to sheltered and domestic scenes slides easily into modern times. Recently an auto mechanic, explaining the proper care of my car, pointed out (with kind intent) that after all I didn't drive it much: "To church, or to the market, or to buy a new dress." He apparently thought he had me figured out, although he didn't know me from Eve.

This mapping out of male and female terrain continues very powerfully in the media. Marshall McLuhan (1967) wrote about television (a gothic form all its own) and brought heroic geography up to date. He compared the horse opera to the soap opera and pointed out that man's world is the frontier while woman's world is the hometown. The blood-and-guts arena of barter and exchange, of fists, swords, and guns where duels are fought, deals are made, and showdowns are a way of life is man's world. It's the traditional ground for traditional heroism. Warriors, businessmen, and athletes resemble horse opera heroes in their harshness and their exercise of raw power.

The world of the soap opera, on the other hand, is a different picture, one filled with anxiety and woe and ambiguous questions of relationship and responsibility. Women's programs are usually set in someone's living room, kitchen, or office. If they stray from these settings, they don't go much further than a restaurant, a hotel or airport lobby, or some other familiar place, all interior settings like the terrain of women in earlier fiction. If women venture outside these settings, they are usually accompanied by—or accompanying—the men in their lives.

The soap opera, even though it takes place in recognizable and familiar scenes, is still only a pale copy of the troubles that take place in everyday settings. Bianca describes the effort it takes for her to visit her parents' home at the end of her work day. She calls it a problem of "reentry." The once-familiar setting is now a household filled with life-support systems, technicians, and nursing personnel. They are all there to sustain her father, who is dying of a progressive degenerative disease. Bianca has to mobilize herself to keep her aging mother from being overwhelmed and to maintain what she can of a loving interaction with her father, who is only a reminiscence of his former self. This she does, with the help of steadfast friends who relieve her so she can have some time off when she is not working and who listen to her grief.

The burden that falls on the caretakers in a family is often a consequence of geography; nearby family members unable or unwilling to place disabled relatives in nursing homes can see familial settings transformed into endurance contests. Further complications arise from the mobility that places other family members miles away. Absent family members spend their time traveling back and forth when they can, or they make decisions long-distance and hope they were right.

We have all known women who behaved heroically within
a narrow landscape of neighborhood and family. Like Thoreau on
Walden Pond, they saw the world played out on their small stage.
Within the narrow geography of their lives, people committed adultery, sickened, killed themselves, were killed, betrayed those who
loved them, or mysteriously disappeared forever. These women experienced the same mixture of ugly and glorious moments that visit
the lives of the more elevated and noble people. But the geography
of these moments was private and miniature and did not measure
up to the definition of public heroism. Private heroism, known to
only a few people or even only to one other person, is often
unremarked.

But heroism it is. For these unpublic women, every day is an
ingenious battle to maintain their humanity and the dignity of
those they love. They steadfastly persevere with a vigorous and
homely courage that makes the marble Pietà appear impatient. It's
too easy to dismiss these domestic dramas—played out on a small
stage, drably costumed, lacking scenic design and background
music, shared only by intimates—as trivial and to consider these
women inconsequential. They have a language of shrugs, sighs,
and smiles, and their audience consists of their children, their sisters, and women neighbors, equally mute and unheard. But who
can measure the inspiration and example that their heroism inspires in people around them?

One of the toxic consequences of women's geographical restriction is that many women collude in regarding their own sphere
of activities as minor and unimportant. Shrugs, qualifying phrases,
and belittling adjectives accompany the apologetic manner in
which they introduce their ideas or opinions. They have a "little"
suggestion, or "just" an idea, or they "only" thought of something
(Moers, 1976). Both the "*style* (hesitant, qualified, question-posing)
and *content* (concern for the everyday, the practical, and the interpersonal)" of the way women talk "is typically undervalued by men
and women alike." (Belenky, Clinchy, Goldberger and Tarule,
1986, p. 17). A miniature and bounded self-portrait, appropriate for
fitting into cramped spaces, leads some women arbitrarily to dis-
qualify themselves from arenas where they could make important
statements about important issues.

A restrictive physical geography can also imprison a woman's spirit. Too often a woman believes the common dictate that her manual dexterity should situate her at the typewriter but not at the operating table, or behind the teller's window but not the bank president's desk. A battle against such restrictions is fought around the kitchen table when the little girl talks of her day in school, in the classroom when the student discovers that she is also capable of excelling in arithmetic, in the therapist's office when the young woman learns that she need not settle for a minor position, and when the older woman masters skills she had been taught were unfeminine, like deciding on her own budget and balancing her own checkbook.

Women still are substantially denied entrance into attractive, well-paying jobs and use up too much energy in the struggle against these restrictions. A woman reporter who covers sports, business, or politics needs the same access to locker rooms, boardrooms, and hotel rooms that her male counterparts have. But before she can sit down to write, she has to fight for admittance. If she chooses a more traditionally female area—such as society happenings—she encounters few such geographical barriers.

For years this perspective has hampered women at all levels of accomplishment. Linda Ellerbee (1987, p. 127) tells a story about the poet Edna St. Vincent Millay, who was the only woman to receive an honorary degree from New York University in 1937. Millay was told that "while she would be dining with the Chancellor's wife, the other recipients of honorary degrees, all men, would be attending a separate dinner at the Waldorf Astoria."

Patricia told me casually one day about her experience. She was one of the first women admitted to an all-male college, and at graduation she was the class valedictorian. But instead of the customary plaque given to the male valedictorians before her, she was given a *charm* for her bracelet. At the time, she didn't think much about it. Only later did she realize the tacit message. Fortunately, this could not happen today without raising a storm of protest from men and women alike.

Hardship and Heroic Geography

Hardship is the greatest inspiration for heroic response to geographical limits. Eula Hall founded the Mud Creek Clinic in the heart of Kentucky's coal mining country. She has only an eighth-grade education, yet she runs a clinic that treats fifty to seventy-five patients a day. Eula attends to her patients' emotional needs as well as their physical disabilities. She picks people up and takes them either to the clinic or to government offices to apply for their benefits. She brings food and medicine to those who can't leave their homes (Kilborn, 1991).

Maria Elena started to work at age five processing shrimp: "Standing up on a big wooden crate, competing with grownups on how to learn to do the job . . . I would do this mostly during the night. This way I could help provide food" (Buss, 1985, p. 249). Later, she dived for potatoes in the dangerous pond outside a warehouse where they were washed, cadged for any other kind of food she could get for herself and her family, begged for bananas on the rough docks, and hopped boxcars to steal pineapples.

Venturing outside assigned turf is dangerous, but desperation and pride are powerful motivators. We spoke of Rosa Parks, the "patron saint of civil rights." When she wouldn't give up her seat to a white man and move to the rear of the bus where African-Americans were supposed to sit, she was arrested. But her act also led to a thirteen-month boycott that resulted in the Supreme Court outlawing segregation on public vehicles (Shipp, 1988).

History tells us that some women disguised themselves as men in order to escape their limitations as females. We see a similar approach today, when "dressing for success" requires women who invade the business and professional worlds to wear the same costume—suit, shirt, and tie—that their male colleagues wear—with a skirt, of course.

Masculine-style dress has historically allowed some women access to places where the possibilities for heroic action match their own energy and ideals. This does not always guarantee safety, however. For example, the doughty Penthesilia, woman warrior of the Trojan War, was killed by Achilles. After her death, when he saw that she was a woman, he regretted killing so valiant and beautiful an opponent—but that didn't stop him from raping her corpse. Joan of Arc was burned as a witch after dressing in male armor and claiming that she was divinely inspired (thereby bypassing male churchly authority).

Many women put on male attire and fought and died alongside their men in the Revolutionary and Civil Wars, but we hear little of them. And what we do hear describes them as dubious characters; they are often simply dubbed "camp followers." But they did much more than follow; they provided some of the essential services not offered by the armies. They served as cooks, laundresses, and water carriers. Some of them worked as nurses in the crude military hospitals. Some were spies, others were messengers. Deborah Sampson actually served as a soldier for two and a half years before her sex was discovered after she became ill. Later, Congress granted her *husband* a pension because he was "the widower of a revolutionary soldier" (Evans, 1989, p. 52).

Colonial women signed and circulated pledges to stop drinking tea, refused to buy British goods, and spun and wove their own cloth. Within their domestic territory, these women were behaving politically, and both England and the colonists knew it. Embedded in the geography of home and family, these women found ways to make their allegiance known beyond the familiar walls.

Much of the political activity of women begins with their interest in improving locally or personally oppressive conditions. Women's involvement in eighteenth-century France began with food riots and market disturbances, ominous precedents to the French Revolution (Randall, 1982).

Women moved into public geography by applying the same skills they had developed in running their households to public need. They formed voluntary associations where women banded together to deal with the deficiencies of their communities. As we have seen, this is a form of heroism characteristic of women: individual women claim new territory and begin enlisting other women to help.

For example, in the early 1800s, women founded seminaries to improve the education of women and enable them to move out of their parlors (or more likely, back bedrooms) and become self-supporting teachers. Emma Willard sat in on boys' examinations so that she could teach her female students subjects, like mathematics and science, they would not otherwise learn. Later she was one of the founders of the Troy Female Seminary, one of whose students, by the way, became the noted abolitionist and suffragist Elizabeth

Cady Stanton (Stephenson, 1986). Other women's associations worked for reform of womens' property rights, alleviation of prostitution, construction of orphanages, and the abolition of slavery.

Women were among the most energetic and untiring participants in the abolitionist struggle to free the slaves. In order to serve the abolitionist cause, many women traveled far from home to make speeches recruiting new members. When they left the familiar geography of home and family, women courted opposition and disapproval. They met criticism and censure not only of their cause but of them for leaving their kitchens and darning needles.

Actually, their critics were right to be worried. The vigorous and enterprising women who began by working for abolition soon saw the obvious application of their intelligence and energy to their own purposes. Many of the same women who developed political effectiveness and know-how in the abolitionist cause went on to work for the suffragist movement.

Although women's political activism begins in personal geography, it doesn't stop there; it crosses a threshold, an entry point where women discover their political backbone. Many women activists then go on to issues of the larger communities of city, state, nation, and world. The Women's Christian Temperance Movement, for example, expanded its agenda to include prison reform, child labor laws, and women's suffrage. The General Federation of Women's Clubs left behind its original interest in literary events to concern itself with social service and reform (Randall, 1982).

The young women mill workers who roomed together in the boarding houses of textile towns protested both their inadequate wages and long working hours. They were pioneers in labor organization and political action. Over one hundred years later, another woman, Alice Paul, was instrumental in organizing working women into unions (Stephenson, 1986).

Presently, women are motivated by deteriorating conditions in their neighborhoods, declining academic standards in their local schools, industrial pollution, and the issue of control over local health services. They are battling for neighborhood reform.

Louise Stanley started a modern squatters' movement in Brooklyn ("Heroes for Hard Times," 1988). She organized "break-ins" where squatters would invade and inhabit condemned city-owned apartment buildings. Once in residence, they began to rehabilitate the buildings with the help of neighbors, who supplied water and electricity. Finally, after the squatters' struggles with city officials aroused public sympathy, the city allocated almost three million dollars to help with the rehabilitation work!

Barbara Williams is a security guard at P.S. 94 in the Bronx. But her influence extends further than the front door. She is the "matriarch of P.S. 94 and its surrounding territory," dispensing advice and encouragement to students—and even to parents, who call her when "they need to find a baby sitter, when their child is in trouble or when they are feeling alone or broke or trapped or all three and they want to talk" (Rimer, 1990, p. A1).

Other women are using intimate geography to confront personal trauma. Norma has organized a group of women who were sexually molested as children to meet in each other's homes to discuss and resolve some of the unfinished feelings that still intrude into their present lives. She remarked that although she thought she had resolved most of her injuries, these meetings had uncovered an emotional residue, something unresolved from their original trauma. Speaking in this group was an intermediate step out of private shame.

Conclusion

Women's heroism has a practical connection to human relationship and context that endows even geographically limited actions with timeless significance. Historically too often confined to everyday settings, women have risen to heights of endurance and courage. Their heroism, occurring in a familiar geography, often has an ordinariness that discourages recognition. But this ordinariness must not discourage *attention*; women's heroism has potent social consequences.

There is a geography of the spirit that knows no difference between male and female. This larger geography is the proper geography of heroism.

EIGHT

Family Ties

Men were the keepers of the adventurous spirit while women
were the ones who made and kept homes, families, roots.
—Ellen Goodman, *Turning Points*

For generations, the family has been the vital connection that filters society's injunctions down to its individual members. It is a cultural womb, nourishing and giving birth to the heroic ambitions of society's sons and daughters. Yet, paradoxically, many early legends totally disregarded the developmental contributions of the family.

Consider this: Adam and Eve had neither infancy nor adolescence. Their divine Father brought them to life fully grown by simply willing them into existence. Family trouble began outside of Eden, when Adam and Eve had children of their own in human fashion. Until they left Eden, they had no family experience. Since the prime way to learn to be a parent is to observe one's own parents, Adam and Eve raised their children under a great handicap.

In early Greek legends as well, many divine or heroic figures were born as completely grown adults. In some myths, just as in the Bible, such creation is the exclusive ability of a divine and powerful father. Prometheus, remember, created the first man; Zeus vengefully created Pandora, the first woman, in order to punish Prometheus. Athena sprang, fully grown, from the head of Zeus, and Venus arose, already exquisite, from the oceanic womb where she had been conceived. Jason's adventures in search of the Golden Fleece include his sowing a handful of dragon's teeth and harvesting a crop of armed warriors. Mind, beauty, and might totally by-passed both fetal dependency on the mother and childhood dependency on the family.

Today, we could argue, almost the opposite prevails. The astronomical cost of raising and educating children prolongs the period of their dependency on parental support. The traditional family—where Dad works and Mom stays home to look after the kids, who will cheerfully bounce into apple-cheeked freshman athleticism and sophomore cheerleading—is a rosy-colored image from the past.

Nowadays family burdens are heavy. The main weight of caring for the household, the children, and aging parents still falls primarily on the shoulders of the woman in the family, whether she is working or not. For some young women, giving precedence to their own goals is a painful option.

The competing demands are exemplified by Rachel, a bright, energetic, and idealistic woman who works hard at a job where she can set her own hours. What this so-called freedom boils down to is that she has to coordinate her clients and then, like a circuit rider, set up a route that includes marketing, visiting her mother and supervising her care in a residential center, exploring colleges for her high school daughter, devoting time to charity work, and trying to live a satisfying life with her husband and friends. She wouldn't want less. Her philosophy of life, she says, can be summed up in one word: "Whew!" She had not thought of her life as heroic, however, until she told me during a therapy session of a conversation with her daughter. Lynn is a real powerhouse; she made good grades, was a class officer, tutored elementary school students, and was a solid contributing member in her classes. This particular time Rachel had expressed admiration of Lynn's accomplishments. To her surprise, Lynn responded by saying how much she had learned from her mother's example. To Lynn, Rachel was a hero, and when she told me of this, Rachel found out that I too considered her heroic.

In some ways, though, Rachel is lucky. The high cost of living has forced some children who can no longer afford to live on their own to return to live with mom and dad. Aged parents have become an economic and emotional burden. The alarming rise in reported incidents of abuse of children—and also of elderly parents—testifies to the strains to which crowded families are subject.

Homeless old people can be seen wandering with shopping carts and plastic bags full of their ragged belongings. Cast-off children loiter on unfriendly city sidewalks. Homelessness among women has increased eightfold since the 1950s (Rossi, 1990). The increased dependence on urban hospital emergency rooms as the only source of medical care for poor families is yet more evidence of the unbearable load on fragile family systems. Sometimes even decent fathers sicken under the sight of their ill-clothed and ill-fed families and simply give up and leave. Women exert themselves heroically every day to keep families together. But with poverty as a daily companion, the fibers that keep a family together grow as threadbare as their clothing.

The Devaluation of Motherhood

Beginning with the early creation stories, maternal influence has been belittled and, in some cases, nullified. In spite of the obvious centrality of women in childbirth, Greek and Biblical accounts of the lives of heroes either diminish the mother's role or promote her displacement. In one myth after another, the mother of the hero is set aside or done away with entirely. The hero emerges immaculately from a water jug, a basket floating in the river, or a lump of clay. In one famous tale of childhood, the hero materializes from a batch of gingerbread dough and, true-to-form, immediately deserts his "parents."

These myths carried a clear message for the families of early times. Boys and girls had to mature quickly in Greek and Biblical times. Life expectancy was short for both sexes. Men left home in their teens to become the warriors their aggressive city-states needed, and women had to begin early to bear future soldiers and future mothers of soldiers. Mothers served a supportive function, but then they were to step aside. The maternal bond, if too strong, hobbled the male hero.

Until recently (still true in many places, unfortunately), giving birth *was* a supreme act of heroism. The clumsy and septic conditions accompanying childbirth made it very dangerous. Silent witnesses to the risks—skeletons found in ancient cemeteries reveal that the death rate of young Greek women of childbearing age was disproportionately high (Pomeroy, 1975).

It was feared that acknowledgment of the centrality of the maternal relationship would encourage emotional bondage; the threats posed by such an inescapable tie seemed to require a thorough separation. This fear is more than ancient history. Centuries later, Philip Wylie was still trying to disentangle a generation that he felt was too dominated by their mothers. He wrote that pregnancy and childbirth are "no more of a hardship than, say, a few months of a benign tumor plus a couple of hours in a dental chair" (1959, p. 47).

The family themes within our myths reiterated that women should be subordinate. Women were seen as untrustworthy and deceitful. Independent or unpredictable behavior was mistrusted. Greek dramatists consistently portrayed women as "vindictive, jealous, petty toward each other." Wolf (1984, p. 179) argues that such deformity of character would likely be found in anyone of good energy who is denied full exercise of her or his faculties and who is "driven out of public life, chased back to home and hearth." Women, presumably unfit to govern and ineligible for battle, were valuable only for their ability to bear children—and to let them go. A tragic echo of this same set of priorities can be discerned in Nazi Germany, where women—at an early age—were exhorted to bear children for the greater good of the Reich.

Today, technology has given women unprecedented options about childbearing. The exercise of choice, always present in heroic decision, has increased for women. I know a young woman who chose to get pregnant again after two harrowing experiences: first, she attended her infant daughter as she died slowly of a progressive disease, and second, she underwent a painful abortion late in her next pregnancy because the malformed fetus had died in utero. In our therapeutic work, she went back to those painful years and asked herself if she could bear the fear and sorrow that would surely accompany another pregnancy. We confronted all the messages she was getting from other people in her family, particularly her mother's dire predictions and her husband's dear wish for another child. And what about her own wishes and apprehensions? She decided to get pregnant. Then much of our work centered around helping her tolerate the uncertainty that dogged her pregnancy. Even now, with a healthy infant, she anxiously counts the days and months that parallel the short life of her dead daughter in an anxious need to pass beyond that one last hurdle. Nevertheless, she says she is proud of having made her choice. Heroism, nothing less.

Woman: Envied and Feared

Beginning with the obvious inequality between mother and son, women's power seems incredibly threatening. The ethos that supported a hero's separation from home and family could also serve to disavow an unwelcome sense of dependency. Dinnerstein proposes that even today the initial relationship between mother and son profoundly distorts the status of women in our society. A woman, she points out, "is the will's first, overwhelming adversary. . . . In our first real contests of will . . . the victor is always female" (1976, p. 166). Women's early centrality in child-rearing is continued by the contemporary predominance of women as elementary school teachers, public school nurses, and administrative personnel. This inequality of boys to grown women leaves men with a need to reconstitute the power differential, for example, by making women wait for centuries just to get the vote.

The mythological horror story about a son's attachment to his mother is the tale of Oedipus, the unfortunate king of Thebes, who killed his father and married his mother. Centuries later, Freud used the Oedipus legend to warn about the dangerous nature of the mother/son bond. To be called a "mama's boy" is an insult at any age. It is common now to be both frightened by this bond and, like whistling in the dark to keep up one's courage, to make jokes about it. On the light side, Bruce Jay Friedman, in his novel *A Mother's Kisses* (1964), invented a Jewish mother whose philosophy of mothering is summed up in her promise to her son, "I'll give you so much care you won't know whether you're coming or going"—so much care, in fact, that she takes up residence in the same town in which her son, Joseph, has just enrolled in college.

Jealousy, dependency, and attraction constitute a complex and contradictory mix of emotions. In grown men, the conflict rages between their attraction to women and their independent status. In present-day cultures, where the mother is the dominant figure in the rearing of her young son and where there is no clearcut demarcation of when a male reaches independent adult status, harshness or brutality to women appears to be a common characteristic (McClelland, 1975). It is as if a young man must prove to his friends—by acting scornful and distant to women in general—that he has outgrown his mother. Hypermasculinity becomes a logical assertion of independence. By spurning tender interaction with any woman, the young man proves how strong he is. Women then become either the victim to be rescued or the victim to be brutalized and ignored—or both. Either way, women come out the losers, and men come out with a choice between being heroes or brutes.

The harshness of separation appears to be related to the ambiguity of detachment. Macho posturing appears less prominent in those cultures where ceremony clearly marks the young boy's entrance into adulthood. Where the transition to masculine independence is recognized, there is less need for continual reassurance about independence (McClelland, 1975).

In our modern societies, where coming-of-age rituals are rare, we may find some compensatory declarations of manhood. But they are often civil rather than religious, and they usually mark adulthood for both sexes: getting a driver's license, graduating from school or college, being old enough to drink, vote, or serve in the armed forces.

But these legalistic civil recognitions have little to say about human relationships, except in terms of individual competence and fiscal or moral responsibility for serious consequences, if any. The writings of Robert Bly and Sam Keen counsel men's need for experiences that help them reclaim a sense of masculinity (Bly, 1990; Keen, 1991).

In his classic work *The Myth of the Birth of the Hero*, Rank (1959) proposed that a critical evolution in the life of the male hero required him to sever connections between himself and his family. Rank believed that this separation was a crucially important developmental task for the growing child and also for society, whose progress depends on the sequential disowning and surpassing of each generation by the succeeding generation.

Men's struggles to separate from their mothers were repeatedly mythologized as prerequisites to heroic status. The company of women was to be outgrown quickly and thereafter shunned. The bias against perceiving heroism in women had some basis in the need to assert male independence. Women could not be heroes; therefore, they were irrelevant to him for whom heroism was a goal.

In many hero tales, fate forces the hero to separate from his family. Perhaps he is born to noble parents, disowned by them in infancy, and exposed to die in the wilderness. He is subsequently found and raised by others, whom he takes to be his true parents—like the unfortunate Oedipus. Or a hero of humble birth may be taken into a royal household, where he proves, through native virtue, to be a redeemer, champion, or avenger, like Moses. In either case, it is clearly implied that separation from the family of origin is prerequisite to male heroic destiny.

Stories of the birth and childhood of the hero often contain an element of magical, but ominous, portent that justifies the separation. For example, it was because of a dire prediction that he would kill his father and marry his mother that the infant Oedipus was sent away in the first place. Joseph's jealous brothers separated him from his doting father, but their betrayal actually sent him on the path to his extraordinary destiny.

Separation has practical advantages for the traditional male hero. After all, those who know him and his family well are less likely to recognize the heroic nature of someone who grew up next door. Actual separation from the family hearth, where humble everyday activities take place, is the most obvious way to leave the humdrum and enter into enterprises of scope and courage. Women, confined to the domestic scene, seem automatically denied access to any heroic possibilities outside the family.

Women in heroic legends are primarily characters whose roles were essentially determined by their *attachment* to the heroes. The fact that their bravery often required them to defy their original families underscores their dilemma. It appears that women separate from their families only to form alliances with heroes, as occurs in the legends of Medea and Ariadne. But, as in these two examples, defiance of family was not tolerated in women; it often ended in tragedy. On the other hand, definace is taken for granted in male heroes and is often generously rewarded.

Overprotective Mothers

Other legends show different ways of extricating the male hero from his family of origin, from women, and from aged parents. One famous Greek myth centers around the futility of a mother's protectiveness. Thetis, the mother of Achilles, the famous hero of the Trojan War, tried to keep him safe from harm or injury in combat. At his birth she dipped him into the river Styx to make him physically invulnerable. Later, to keep him from going to war, she dressed him as a woman and tried to conceal him among a group of women at their weaving. But Odysseus, the clever schemer, went among the women with a basket of yarn in which he had concealed various weapons. Achilles, all male, gave himself away by being the only "maiden" interested in the weapons rather than the yarn.

Even after Achilles had gone to fight at the gates of Troy, Thetis went to Vulcan, the divine blacksmith, for a suit of armor that would protect Achilles. Poor Achilles. Although his mother, Thetis, did her best to make him invincible, she forgot that the spot where she had been holding him as she dipped him into the river had not been touched by the magic waters, inadvertently leaving him with an Achilles' heel—the dangerous gift of too much mother love.

The implication here is familiar; the mother must be prepared to lose her son so he may follow his heroic quest. These tales warned that it was unwise for the male hero to remain with his family because this would result in a kind of psychological dwarfism and diminish his heroic destiny.

Many of these myths originated as parts of epic poems and histories presented at banquets to the ruling military class, to those enterprising men who waged wars and to those women whose presence at such celebrations was derivative and auxiliary. Severing family connections and shouldering the more important allegiance to glory and to empire were acts that fit the needs of the caesars, the senators, and the generals. True, the warriors may have been born of women, but they quickly distanced themselves from that relationship.

Undoing the Maternal Bond

Repudiating the connection between women and birth or the bond between mother and son is, in one myth after another, like cutting off an embarrassing relationship. Mother love in the Bible finds its noblest expression in a woman's willingness to surrender her child for her or his own good. Moses is placed in the bullrushes at the wish of his unselfish mother, so that Pharaoh's daughter can find him and he will not be killed in the general slaughter of Jewish firstborn male babies. The real mother demonstrates her love before Solomon by giving up her claims to her child rather than seeing the infant divided "fairly" by being cut in half.

An outstanding Greek version of the partial success of a maternal bond, albeit with a daughter, is the legend of Demeter, the goddess of fertility, and her daughter, Persephone. Persephone is abducted by Hades, the god of the underworld. Demeter searches for her, making the the whole earth barren until her daughter is restored. After Persephone returns safely, Demeter teaches the citizens of Eleusis the secret rites that ensure the continued fruitfulness of the earth, a reminder of the early connection between goddesses and fertility.

Greek mothers could learn from the story of Demeter "how much of motherhood is loss" (Downing, 1981, p. 39). But there is an additional implication. Demeter was rescuing a daughter, and a daughter promises the continuation of fertility—subliminal instruction for all Greek mothers and daughters. The story of Demeter and Persephone emphasized the sequence of fertility, nurturance, and devotion that the Greeks wanted from their women.

Centuries later, Paul Goodman, novelist and critic, echoed this paternalistic philosophy. He reassured young women that they need not aspire to any higher function than the simple act of giving birth: "the problems I want to discuss . . . belong primarily, in our society, to the boys: how to be useful and make something of oneself. A girl does not *have* to, she is not expected to 'make something' of herself. Her career does not have to be self-justifying, for she will have children, which is absolutely self-justifying, like any other natural or creative act. With this background, it is less important, for instance, what job an average young woman works at till she is married" (1956, p. 13).

But this self-justification alarmed Philip Wylie into warning that this perspective had a sinister downside. Antedating Susan Faludi's (1991) examples of "backlash" by more than thirty years, Wylie considered the reverence for motherhood unhealthy. He believed that (in the United States at least) such reverence had degenerated into a maudlin sentimentality that he called "megaloid momworship," and he cautioned that this was not good for mothers or sons. He argued that mothers would be encouraged to be petulant and shallow tyrants: "Today, while decent men struggle for seats in government with hope of saving our Republic, mom makes a condition of their election the legalizing of Bingo" (Wylie, 1959, p. 187). Amazing? Thirtysome years ago, when he wrote this, the choices for all but the most remarkable women too often were being either virgin or crone, Cinderella or dear old mom. Obviously, Wylie deplored this, as would any spirited woman.

Nobody would claim that staying mother-bound is good for heroic offspring, female or male. More to the point, it isn't good for the heroic nature of mothers either, who confront a maternal paradox. While our myths advocate that the contemporary mother be closely, almost exclusively connected to her family, she is required to yield them up to other more valid undertakings. Many people continue to view mothers as convenient characters primarily devoted to temporary relationships that are inferior to other loyalties.

So women try to unravel a chronic double bind. On the one hand, the old injunction claims that motherhood is a sufficient reason for her existence, and her role in the world is to support the heroics of the men in her life. Additionally, the reduction of woman to mother has led to the conclusion that motherhood somehow subdues the inventive spirit in women, or at least makes it unnecessary. Even as late as 1957, childbearing was used to explain why women are "less creative" than men (Vare and Ptacek, 1988).

Nowadays, we have myths of our own, variations on the classic predicament. Sociologists and psychologists worry that mothers will fall victim to the "empty nest" syndrome after their grown children leave home. They warn this may be the inevitable consequence of the end of a woman's nurturing years. Actually, such an eventuality would not be surprising in a society where, until recently, women have neither been offered nor permitted viable and creative alternatives.

However, many women are energetically contradicting this contemporary bit of mythology. Some mothers describe feelings of relief and liberation when they can stretch their own wings in the now roomier, empty nest. They can begin to fly away too. Remember, when the nest is empty the mother, too, is free to soar. Research interviews suggest that when women can look beyond their families for satisfaction and accomplishment, the myth of the empty nest syndrome proves untrue: "I sometimes worried that I was unnatural, so I didn't really like to talk about it. You know, when you hear all around you that women are pining for their children, you feel as if there's something wrong with you—that you're not a natural mother if you don't" (Rubin, 1979, p. 26).

Placing good old mom on a pedestal not only elevates her; it also severely restricts her movement. In apparently loving confinement the mother's pedestal eventually *becomes* the empty nest.

Mothers and Wives

It wasn't just the heroic son who left home; heroic husbands also left the family to pursue more noble paths. So the wife, as well as the mother, was left to serve as a humble counterpart to the adventuresome men of the family. Women's role as wives was to conserve and defend the property and reputations of their husbands. Francis Bacon summed it up when he said, "Wives are young men's mistresses, companions for middle age, and old men's nurses."

Penelope embodies this feminine ideal. She waits patiently for her husband, Odysseus, while he takes the long way home from the Trojan War—dallying with Nausicaa, Circe, and Calypso and listening to the Sirens' song. Odysseus' fame comes from his adventures away from home and family; Penelope's, on the other hand, comes from her loyal attachment to her absent husband in the face of great pressure. Dido and Ariadne suffered their abandonment in exemplary fashion, appreciating that Aeneas and Theseus, of course, had more important things to do than stay with them once they had outlived their usefulness. They were good little girls to the end.

Like Penelope during the Trojan War, the English wife during the British civil war was a useful creature. Protecting the assets and possessions of her husband, whether he was lord of the manor or humble shopkeeper, she guarded and maintained his property, family, and estate while he was fighting (Fraser, 1984).

Men's freedom to leave home and family, whether they were summoned by their kings or motivated by their own idealism, has historically sustained the ambitions of empires and martial nations—and *it* in turn has been sustained by women. For centuries, women have heroically tried to preserve a way of life and a network of relationships in the face of disruption and disrespect.

Society has been reluctant to acknowledge the heroism of women who conserve and maintain what already exists. But why not recognize the importance of these tasks? Surely this kind of heroism involves the risk of personal injury and ostracism; it requires stamina to endure the often solitary struggle; and it calls for the ability to bravely look at the present and to imaginatively envision the future.

Dolley Madison, fleeing from the White House in the War of 1812, delayed her flight long enough to gather and take with her the documents and paintings she believed essential to the heritage of the young United States. Colonial and homesteading wives were tireless geniuses at supporting and extending the revolutionary idealism of the founding "fathers."

Our contemporary society has produced a new twist on this theme by creating a new generation of women as independent conservators: single mothers and the daughters of aged or frail parents. Through a variety of causes—widowhood, divorce, desertion—45 percent of working women are without partners. Of the women raising children without a partner, 35 percent fall below the poverty line (Hewlett, 1986).

Parents are living longer and are often in poor health. We are finally aware of the tragedies of single daughters who are solely accountable for the care of those who took care of them when they were young.

My patient, Nancy, typifies the modern woman's dilemma. She is a single mother raising a son and a daughter with very little financial support from her former husband. She is also the only child of two aged parents. Her father is no longer able to drive, and her mother's health is precarious. Nancy's daily routine begins with getting her kids off to school and making a quick phone call to her parents to see what she needs to pick up for them on her way home from work. She also has to deal with her former husband, whose bitterness injures and upsets the children on their weekend visits with him. When they come home, she says, the first few hours are spent "just putting them back together."

Another patient, Grace, works with a group of caretakers (mostly women) that meets weekly to support each other through the hardships of twenty-four hour responsibility for infirm parents. These people do not have the money either to place their parents in protected residences or to hire help at home. The group shares with each other tips on how to cope with the pressures of this commitment. They give each other simple, practical advice on how to take care of themselves in the face of sometimes unrelenting demands and discuss any community services that might relieve some of the burden. Grace, whose parents both died when she was quite young, says she is awed by the incredible patience and ingenuity of these people. For her, the group is one way to understand and confront some of the issues about aging parents that she herself could not experience personally.

There are other women who do not join groups, who persevere alone. Janice went through weeks of depressing attempts to find effective care for her ninety-two-year-old mother, who lived miles away and stubbornly maintained that she was entirely capable of living alone. To Janice, it was quite evident that her mother was not as capable as she claimed. This is a fairly common predicament. It would have been simpler just for Janice to find a nursing home and insist that her mother be cared for there.

Although Janice was concerned about getting adequate care for her mother, she also wanted to respect her mother's insistence on remaining in her familiar neighborhood, personally overseeing her finances, doing her own grocery shopping, and visiting her old hangouts. In other words, Janice was as much concerned with honoring her mother's unique sense of personhood as she was with the practical arrangements. It took great courage and effort to keep her mother out of institutional care. In addition to arranging for a regular visiting attendant, keeping an eye on her mother's finances, phoning often, visiting whenever she could, Janice also implicitly accepted the fact that she would have to live with the constant worry that something could go wrong. But she accepted this worry as a fitting price for her mother's satisfaction. Janice did not view this as heroic. But May Sarton (1966), in her poem "The Walled Garden at Clondalkin," knows all about the "patient human ways" of ordinary people doing simply what they think is right, and she honors their "common and heroic days" (p. 100).

Not all aged parents are frail, though. In Glen Cove, New York, grandmothers patrol the grounds of their housing project to reduce the drug trafficking there. Their weapons are notebooks and walkie-talkies. One grandma, Lena Pinkney, is barely five feet tall, but she says, "I'm just short, that's all, not small by a long shot" (Winerip, 1988, p. D5).

Conclusion

Our concept of heroism has traditionally valued the exploits of heroes who distance themselves from home and family. We have not recognized the heroism of women who did not unravel kinship ties.

These women have preserved life, home, and spirit with quiet and unostentatious determination, using needle and thread, broom and washcloth, cutting out scraps of pictures to hang on ugly walls, whispering stories of greatness and hope as they put their children to bed. Within these family relationships, women have behaved heroically, risking their lives to create new life, nurturing those already born or those who have sickened or been injured, and confronting those who threaten the integrity of their homes.

Women are becoming aware that their inventiveness and courage have relevance to the world beyond their families. Single or partnered, they are centrally important to the welfare—indeed, to the continued existence—of the family, which remains a critical component of the society at large. Although the struggles have silenced and disheartened many, a generation of heroic women has emerged who have met hardship with courage and hard work. Even better, many of them articulate the unequal and unrealistic legacy of women as family caretakers and the inadequacy of structured institutions to recognize and support their struggles.

NINE

Disquieting Heroism

Life, misfortunes, isolation, abandonment, poverty, are bat-
tlefields which have their heroes; obscure heroes, sometimes
greater than the illustrious heroes.
—Victor Hugo, *Les Miserables*

Heroism has a bleak side—stained by death, pain, and injury. Some individuals who attend to these human vulnerabilities are considered heroic and receive great accolades, like Mother Theresa and Albert Schweitzer. On the whole, though, ministrations to vulnerability have not received the praise accorded to more flamboyant forms of heroism. Women's heroism, often carried out in services that *recognize* and *tend* to human vulnerability, may be too uncomfortable a reminder of the bloody underside of heroic exploits. Phillips (1984, p. 13) acknowledges this, observing that "the beginning of civilization seems to require the seizure of religious power by male gods, in order to break the ties of humanity to blood, soil and nature."

Uneasy about our own vulnerabilities, we are uncertain whether to attend to them or transcend them. We clearly prefer that our heroes disdain *their* vulnerabilities. For example, a recent spate of movies has presented us with heroes who are not even flesh and blood. When *they* are injured, they don't bleed; they melt down to reveal an interior made up of electronic circuitry. We call upon our human heroes, too, to ignore their physical limitations. In a recent Olympics, the crowds actually booed track star Carl Lewis when he did not put all his effort into winning a certain event (after already

139

winning several). He was pacing himself, and wisely so, because he was aiming for a record in a major track event coming up.

The actual fact is that although Superman may astound, in the everyday world heroic work is done by vulnerable *human* heroes. The human hero is not at all sure of victory, and it is mortal vulnerability that makes human action heroic. We earthlings may yearn toward the divine, but those hopes shrink uneasily when we experience our own limitations. The hero's action, conquering dangers that would immobilize or defeat the rest of us, resolves this paradox for a moment—and for that moment, mortality and immortality are in harmony.

Heroic Caretakers of Traditional Heroes

Women have been the carriers and teachers of the minute details of civilized life. They have been the housekeepers, the preparers of food, the makers of vessel and cloth, of clothing and household articles, and the preservers of supplies for the dark winters. They have attended births and deaths, washing and dressing the corpse as well as the newborn, officiating at the beginnings and endings of life and nursing the infants, the sick, and the elderly in between.

More and more women are working, and they still predominate in those occupations and activities that tend to human vulnerabilities. They are the nurses who care for the sick. They are the teachers who deal with the very young (who are also the very messy) in nursery schools and elementary schools. They are the social workers and the counselors who succor and advise the people who don't know where to turn for help. They are the women who come into the deserted office buildings after the important affairs are done; they empty the wastebaskets, wipe the spills off the boardroom tables and CEOs' desks, and clean the executive washrooms.

Women wage quiet battles for the integrity and preservation of the human body and spirit in the face of a preoccupied or hostile universe. Adrienne Rich (1979, p. 205) provides an eloquent description of women's dedicated defense of their world: "It is this activity of world-protection, world-preservation, world-repair—the million tiny stitches, the friction of the scrubbing brush, the scouring cloth, the iron across the shirt, the rubbing of cloth against itself to exorcise the stain, the renewal of the scorched pot, the rusted knife-blade, the invisible weaving of a frayed and threadbare family life, the cleaning up of soil and waste left behind by men and children—that we have been charged to do 'for love,' not merely unpaid, but unacknowledged by the political philosophers."

Throughout history, women have been largely responsible for dealing with the human functions that contradict our concept of heroic immortality. Judith Bardwick kindly gave me an unpublished manuscript in which she observed that men are confronted with the messy details of life—blood, feces, or vomit—often either as a result of accident or of adventurous activity like hunting or combat. But women have consistently attended to elemental human functions and needs; they have been intimately familiar with the grim consequences of illness and physical injury.

Dinnerstein (1976, p. 124) calls woman the "dirty goddess." After all, it's hard to picture a *hero* cleaning a toilet or emptying a bedpan. Think of the detailed stories about the food our astronauts have taken with them into space—and the lack of discussion about disposal of their all-too-human waste. We would actually like to overlook the quiet heroism that provides the important actors of our world with a filled lunchbox or a clean shirt.

Women, as we all know, have been consigned to domestic activities for generations. Drudge or shrew, shrill or mute, women have been the warriors of the ephemeral: food that once consumed leaves no trace, only an inglorious stack of dirty dishes; laundry—or floors—washed and soiled again in a few hours. It is women who carry the world on their shoulders every day, but it is Atlas who gets the glory.

Yes, much of women's contribution has been written in perishables, which are used up and disappear, leaving no artifacts to win the respect and admiration of future generations. Indeed, Dinnerstein (1976) speculates, the devaluation of women's contribution to civilization may come from the circumstance that their prehistoric creativity used perishable materials—grasses, reeds, leather, clay—as its medium. Such materials, unlike the more durable stone tools and weapons of prehistoric men, have rotted away over the centuries. Incidently, may it not also be reasonable to question whether men were the only ones who made the stone tools in the first place?

It is instructive to look at caretakers in the early United States. The gender neutrality of function was certainly evident in the harsh daily life of the American colonies. Women's work, of course, included ministering to the vulnerable. But it went beyond this. Women were indispensable allies in a setting where the satisfaction of basic needs involved hard work. Furthermore, industriousness was a moral value in the colonies. Everybody had to work for the general economic good. Women worked at all sorts of occupations. As Lerner has noted, they ran mills, plantations, tanneries, and shipyards. In addition to "producing cloth and clothing, women were shoemakers, butchers, upholsterers and worked with silver and making guns . . . they were gatekeepers, jail-keepers . . . printers, 'doctoresses,' apothecaries" (1979, p. 17).

Even so, women's *identities* were determined primarily by their relationship to the men in their lives: fathers, husbands, or brothers. Women of the family were not specifically called out by their first names. Their contributions were subsumed under the *family* name, and they remained *personally anonymous*. Their acts of heroism were countless—but uncounted.

The bravery of women's daily lives was equal to—in some cases, almost identical to—that of their husbands, brothers, and sons—and indispensable to the survival of their new country. But heroic acts were not recorded in women's actual names. Molly Pitcher, for example, was actually Mary Ludwig, from Carlisle, Pennsylvania. During the American Revolutionary War, she followed her husband to Valley Forge and worked cooking and washing, as did many other soldiers' wives. These women performed the functions that are presently carried out by an army quartermaster corps. During the battle of Monmouth, on an unusually hot summer's day, she carried water in her pitcher to the thirsty soldiers. She was given the nickname that honored her in terms of her *function*. When her husband, a gunner in the artillery, succumbed to the heat, she took his place and stayed there until the battle was over. Later "Molly Pitcher" became a collective sobriquet given both to the female camp followers that war invites and to the heroic wives who followed their men into battle (*World Book Encyclopedia,* 1960).

Anonymous as they may have been, women in the early United States developed many of the institutions that maintained the homes and sustained the cities. But women were also sensitive to the needs of those who could not support themselves in the harsh environment of new communities. In addition to the conventional function of rearing their own children, they organized schools and orphanages for unfortunate children. They tended the old and the sick. They founded hospitals and worked there as volunteers. They raised money to fund welfare organizations to house and feed the poor and the sick. They did the heroic but unrecognized work that civilized their communities and preserved the territory the male heroes were busy conquering.

The Untraditional Heroism of Women

It is important to accentuate that the hero gives assertive and energetic recognition to the value and dignity of human life. She herself demonstrates to the vulnerable how life must be lived and supports courage in others.

Patricia Levin is a good example. She is a registered nurse, specializing in hospice care. She has four or five patients, all of them terminally ill, all of them at home where they can die in the company of people who love them. Often the patient's family needs as much tending as the invalid. Patricia's job is to safeguard the dignity of the patient and help the family deal with the reality of death. So, it helps *both* family members when, after an ailing father railed at his adolescent son for reminding him to take his medicine, Patricia took his hand and said, "You know, it sounds like your son loves you very much." She knows of their anguish firsthand. She nursed her own father during his losing battle with cancer (Malcolm, 1991).

Simple, of course. We are all witnesses to the heroism of the everyday. I have seen it on the news; a woman with an artificial leg trains to run in a special event for the physically disabled, the Paralympics. I have seen the face of the mother of a profoundly retarded and crippled son, smiling at him as she straightened him in his wheelchair for the thousandth time. I have seen dogged determination at the kitchen stove, where a woman spent her nights baking in order to earn enough to keep her family together while her depressed husband stayed in bed all day, unable to work.

I have heard about an Air Force pilot who was blamed for the crash in which he died. His wife didn't buy the official explanation. She got access to privileged flight data and studied the controls system on her late husband's aircraft. She then sued the large aircraft manufacturer and won. The explanation for the crash was changed from "pilot error" to instrument failure.

I have also read about grandmothers who nightly patrol the housing projects in which they live to try to stop drug users and dealers (Winerip, 1988).

I have known fatally ill women who confronted their own deaths. While dying, they continued as long as they could to focus on the welfare and stability of the families they loved. Each remained in charge of her life and, ultimately, in charge of her death. When someone called one of these women "indomitable," she was amazed that such a grand word could apply to her.

The heroism of these women was often poignantly simple and ordinary. One woman embroidered a pillow with her son's favorite animal on it, another one sent notes of affection to dear friends—from a bed she knew she would never leave. The heroism of those who loved these women was equally impressive; love was expressed in hours of massage, preparation of special favorite foods, reading aloud, and saving up funny stories to tell each other. All of these activities were examples of the transcendence of the human spirit.

Janice came to me because she needed to reconstruct her life after nursing both her son and her husband through debilitating illnesses and deaths. Alone now, she keeps a journal of self-exploration, where she writes of her loss and of her doubts, conversing with her grief and isolation. But shining through these pages is an intrepid spirit. It is the same spirit that supported her through the dark periods with her husband and son. In therapy she learned how to turn that same courage toward her own present need to reenter *life*. She is daring to reach out to the people who remain in her life, courageously risking once again loving their *aliveness* and

joining them—where she belongs. This kind of unpretentious heroism, which rises above tragedy and loss with grace and spirit, is so
commonplace that it is recorded only among those intimates who
witness it.

It takes an artist's eye to perceive the heroes of the everyday.
Everyday heroes populate the stories of Margaret Atwood, Harriet
Doerr, Mary Gordon, Thomas Hardy, Katherine Mansfield, Toni
Morrison, and Alice Walker. Degas, as well as Manet, Van Gogh,
and Picasso, painted them going about their business—making
hats, sitting on a park bench, eating potatoes, shrieking silently in
the midst of carnage. We have walked past them many times, sat
next to them on the bus—and lived with them.

The photographs in *Let Us Now Praise Famous Men* (Agee
and Evans, 1939) show women and men who faced the toil of
scratching a life from exhausted soil, grudging landlords, and impersonal bureaucratic systems. All they want is to get through one
more winter, put together one more meal, endure one more hour—
and yet one more.

But the indomitable spirit *was* there—once. A photograph in
Let Us Now Praise Famous Men shows a scrap of newspaper cut
into a decorative edging for a shelf in the home of a tenant farmer.
His wife had done this as a bride. But now the edging is discolored,
crumpled, and tragic, like the worn face of the woman who made
it, years after her younger hopefulness has eroded. She looks like a
prisoner sentenced to her own life, unhopeful of parole or pardon.

These pictures put a human face on the tragedy that occurs
when the potent heroism of the everyday is not recognized, when
there is no hope of success, and the hero tale seems irrelevant. It is
at this point that an individual may cross the fine line between
persistence and resignation. When a person cannot act from a sense
of improvisation and determination, her existence becomes a steady
grinding down of the human spirit.

What makes the difference between the energy and lyricism
reflected in the letters of a homesteading wife and the wordless
apathy on the face of a tenant farmer's wife? Elinor Stewart filed her
own claim to land in Wyoming in 1909 because she wanted land of
her own in addition to the land she shared with her husband. She
wrote about homesteading, warning that it was not for anyone

afraid of wild animals and lonely hard work. But she also wrote joyfully of the sunsets, the flowers, and the beauty of her home among the blue mountains (Luchetti, 1982). She was an Eve who knew how to live outside of Eden, an Eve recognizable to contemporary women. She knew that she had to *make* an Eden for herself and her family through her own hard work. She saw her plot of land as a God-given opportunity, one that she would have to purchase by sweat, pain, and exhaustion—and she accepted the divine bargain. Her situation was an opportunity she sought, not a punishing judgment. She willed herself to be an agent for change and to create her own garden in the midst of wilderness. She was ready to use all of herself in doing it. She was heroic.

The wife of the tenant farmer or sharecropper had no such heroic vision. Her life was crowded with the grimy necessities of just getting from day to day, and keeping herself and her family clean was more than she could do. She saw herself as powerless to make a difference. She had grown up under similar dispiriting conditions. Choice and ingenuity had been pinched out of her, leaving her crumpled and dry like an empty flour sack or a potato peeling.

The city women who organize tenant's groups, who monitor the corridors of dangerous public schools, who patrol crime-ridden streets in their neighborhoods are also contemporary Eves. They know that sometimes it is up to them and *their* efforts to make their communities more livable, and they are realistic and energetic enough to not wait for a benevolent authority to act. These are the same people who also speak up at city council meetings and demand that authorities take notice. Upstarts they are—like Eve.

Heroic Women: Uneasy Bargains

Heroic women often make uneasy bargains that link human decision and effort with divine ideals. Heroic women risk their personal welfare, their positions, and even their lives in order to support the principles essential to their way of life. Sometimes, like the homesteading wives, they invade unfriendly or forbidden territory and challenge the powers that rule; sometimes (then as now) their heroism involves staying at home, taking a stand there. Research suggests, for example, that in the recent rash of foreclosures of family farms in the Midwest, the farm wife is an essential bulwark; the stability and welfare of the endangered family lies with her. "If she remains strong, the family stays together. If she crumbles, the family will probably dissolve" (Turkington, 1986, p. 18).

In a television interview (NBC, January 26, 1988), Jimmy Breslin, journalist and author, said that Theresa Fisher was the real hero of a teenage interracial fight in Howard Beach, New York, that resulted in the death of one young black man. She saw the attack from her apartment window, called the police, and then got into her car to search for the young man she had seen beaten. Later, she walked into a courtroom filled with hostile neighbors and testified against the assailants. She ignored the enmity this act would bring down on her in order to oppose the prejudice that infected her neighborhood.

It is important to remember that such women do not come easily to their heroic choices. While fictional heroes appear fearless, human heroes may well be afraid. They act in spite of their fear; indeed, some may act because of it. The awareness of vulnerability can lead to cowardice because the possibility for success is more than counterbalanced by the likelihood of defeat. Greek legends and the Bible tell story after story about their gods frustrating the struggles of kings and warriors and humbling them when they grew too arrogant. Great ambition in an ordinary person might bring on a rapid fall.

The frightening prospect of ambition opposed and penalty inflicted can indeed be a chastening influence. Women, especially those who were accomplished and ambitious, have always been in double danger. First, it was arrogant for both women and men to aspire to *divine* skills. One cautionary Greek legend tells of Arachne, a mortal woman who claimed she was as skillful a weaver as the goddess Athena and who dared to challenge the goddess to a contest. Skillful as she was, Arachne lost. As punishment for her hubris, Athena, with an ironic sense of appropriate vengeance, transformed Arachne into a different form of expert weaver—a spider.

For women, though, there was a second form arrogance could take: women could aspire to do the things that *men* did—or to try to influence their world as freely as men did. Over the years proscriptions against such behavior have persisted in various

guises. Some people still advocate that women should settle for the
"natural capacities" they have by simply being female. Somehow
women's natural capacities too often appear like deformities—like
the bound feet of the Chinese women who were not supposed to
move vigorously in any direction.

Heilbrun (1990, p. 30) cites the experience of the poet H. D.
in her analysis with Freud, who told her that "not only did she want
to be a boy, she wanted to be a hero." This was how Freud saw
women who had ambitions beyond what he (and most people of his
time) considered feminine.

Women's fight for personal eligibility for individual positions of eminence has often preceded the fight to change the larger
status quo. One consequence of women's self-effacement is that too
many women still see themselves as ineligible; they see themselves
too often as *supporters* of candidates for important positions rather
than as candidates themselves. Women who challenge the status
quo and define their own agendas are actually inaugurating a giant
healing effort; they perceive the disease in the unfit policies of an
organization or institution. Their criticism is like lancing a boil or
cauterizing a festering sore.

Beverly Carl, a law professor at Southern Methodist University, filed a complaint with the U.S. Department of Labor charging
the university with discrimination against women in "hiring, pro-
motion, retention, compensation, and appointment to prestigious
posts." University officials protested that they didn't understand her
complaint. It wasn't their fault; there simply weren't enough well-
qualified women. Nevertheless, after she filed her complaint, *for the
first time in sixteen years* Professor Carl was not asked to sit on the
Graduate Committee. Professor Carl's action, however, resulted in
salary increases for four women professors and the development of
an affirmative action plan for the university. Herold (1986, p. 11)
compares her and women like her to "aging generals manning the
front lines until fresh troops arrive."

Women executives, physicists, administrators, deans, editors,
football players, stand-up comics, legislators, judges, mechanics,
and astronauts are our modern heroes, venturing beyond familiar
roles and asserting their relevance to prohibited activities. Other
women watch them and then apply what they have learned to their

own lives. Through the heroic experience of exemplary women, other women make connections to the heroic in *their* nature, tailoring *their* talents to the specific challenges they face. Real-life tales filled with obstacles overcome, disasters surmounted, and adversity put to good use encourage us to confront our own handicaps and deal inventively with the restrictions of our own humanity.

Imperfect Heroes

Some hero tales acknowledge the importance—actually, the omnipresence—of human vulnerability by telling of inauspicious beginnings, personal handicap, disability, or disadvantage. These stories have clumsy or disrespected heroes who are cast out, exiled, laughed at. Sometimes the very qualities that led to the hero's rejection may be crucial to the development of the heroic character.

When this kind of heroism is brought to our attention, we find it compelling because it plays itself out—*despite handicap*—in simple acts of courage and ingenuity. This has implicit and powerful relevance to our own lives because we are painfully aware of our own shortcomings. Sometimes these heroic "misfits" can be more inspiring than the flawless heroes whose actions seem out of reach to ordinary folk.

When Rosalind came to see me for therapy, she couldn't exactly put her finger on what troubled her. What was painfully clear, however, was that she wore leg braces because she had polio as a child. She had always had difficulty keeping up with schoolmates during her childhood and adolescence. Now, as a sophomore in college, she still had great trouble keeping up with her fellows as they walked across campus. But she was unwilling to *say* anything about it; she didn't want to ask them to walk more slowly. Not keeping up left her with the same old feeling that she was always on the edge of any group and never quite part of it. Plainly, as she had difficulty telling me—a willing listener—what her problem was, she was reluctant to talk about this problem with her friends. All her life, Rosalind had heroically maintained a "stiff upper lip." As we explored her fear of admitting her disability, she realized that it *was* visible and that she surely wasn't kidding anyone. I pointed out the tremendous courage she had exercised during her childhood trying to keep up with the other kids. Now, however, she needed another form of heroism: to face her fear of speaking forthrightly to her friends, to ask them to match their pace to hers, and not to settle for her chronic feeling of disability and exclusion. She did, and they did, glad to cooperate. They *wanted* to get to know her better, and soon Rosalind's increased contacts with them led to sessions where they, too, could talk of their limitations.

Murray (1960) points out how the suffering of a representative hero can provide us with inspiration. Based on the hero's suffering, we make up the personal myths that are particularly apt for our situations. Bettelheim (1977) echoes this observation when he notes that the message of fairy tales is that struggles in life are inevitable, but they can be overcome by courage and directness. Hero tales that deal with vulnerability do the same for the adult.

There is only minimal solace, as we all know, in learning that someone else's misery is worse than our own. But such knowledge can also be somewhat heartening. The awareness that other women are willing to risk failure encourages us to distinguish between a hopeless cause and one that deserves further pursuit. This is a renewal of the heroic sense of possibility. Instead of bemoaning a loss, we become energized to make another try.

Conclusion

We all need heroes to sustain us in our daily struggles with human vulnerabilities and the disturbing risks of an uncertain existence. Our emphasis on the flair and glitter of traditional heroism ignores the mundane details that are essential supports in our daily lives.

Women heroes in particular define and maintain a sense of vulnerability. They juggle the contradictions between the heroic spirit and the unheroic flesh. They are faced every day with the challenges, injuries, and confrontations of the world.

We must recognize the heroism that addresses unhappiness and pain next door. Heroism also appears in the public schools, where a group of women volunteers develop tutorial reading programs for children for whom English is a second language or where a teacher puts in extra hours devising lessons to help her less prepared students.

We see unpretentious heroism in the hundreds of idealistic young people who devote years to service in underdeveloped countries, constructing irrigation and sewage systems, setting up schools, teaching people how to fight disease and how to grow their own food. We find it in the doctors who volunteer their services on floating hospital ships or motorized caravans that reach people who would otherwise go without medical care.

This kind of heroism acknowledges and nourishes the humanity of the hero. It gives diversity and depth to the courage of our commonplace heroic image. Rooted in the actuality of the vulnerable, it bears an actual relevance to the daily vulnerabilities that complicate our lives.

TEN

Glory Stories

The problems in American folklore . . . are to separate the
folklore of the folk from the fake lore of the industrial man.
—Richard M. Dobson, "Theories of Myth
and the Folklorist," in *Myth and*
Mythmaking, edited by Henry A. Murray

We have become habituated to the buckle and swash of the colorful characters that dominate our news reports and fiction. We devour these media presentations everyday—and we hardly even wonder at them. The media attract us through sensationalism, and then they maintain our appetite by providing more and more of the same inflated, insubstantial diet. One American television producer explained that the British coverage of the Wimbledon tennis matches, where commentary and hype are minimal, were "a little bit sterile for our audience. . . . We have to focus on emotion, be superaggressive and get closer to the action. Reserve and respect are not our way of doing it" (Tavris, 1982, p. 177).

A TV journalist once told me that the cameramen were instructed to film a protest march on a nearby college campus *only* if it got violent. A peaceful demonstration would not be vibrant enough to attract and hold a viewer who sits with remote control in hand, ready to move on to more colorful stuff.

Spectacular action, as defined by the ministers of the media, consistently nudges other less obviously dramatic events to the back pages of newspapers, to the public broadcasting network, or to the early morning programs on radio and television. The front pages of newspapers are usually dominated by reports of bombings, mergers, international conferences, and political skirmishes. Sadly, women figure only rarely in the selected events. The women who do appear in front-page articles or in accompanying photos fade into the background: secretaries, interpreters, or aides, always unnamed, often not even functionally identified. Sometimes the picture of a woman materializes on the front page, a smiling wife accompanying her husband on a diplomatic mission. Not long ago, one newspaper showed a picture of a woman construction worker on page four. *She* was newsworthy because, in the middle of a heat wave, she was wearing a skimpy tank top as she worked. Such reportage simply reinforces the familiar assumption that women may be either decorative or peripheral.

Heroes Make the News, and News Makes the Heroes

As influential as the printed media are in creating a sense of cultural priorities, television is even more powerful. In television, one aspect of an event is spotlighted, while other equally vital components are cast into shadow. This ability is critical; it simplifies experience for millions of viewers and registers the event sharply. Such uncluttered and stark presentation actually *confers existence.*

Television news broadcasts give us both more and less information than we need. In both cases, prior selection of events by directors and cameramen relegates our own perception to a second-hand function, based on preedited data. Photographs, news features, and news clips purport to cover an event and to represent reality, but actually they focus narrowly on a particular circumstance or happening and more often than not, on the men who are central. The preselection process is inevitable, of course, since all communication requires choice. But the result is that one person, somewhere in the control room of the television channel, has preset the priorities on which another person will view the news and make decisions.

Incomplete or slanted as the coverage may be, pictures and print carry a stamp of reality, tangible and hard to disbelieve. It is only natural to trust our own eyes and rely on the information we accumulate. Some of us know that our personal vision has always provided us with a limited apprehension of truth. But our susceptibility is increased now that technicians can retouch photographs, erase and dub videotapes and audiotapes, edit interviews and reports, use quotes out of context, or add an emphasis that was not there in the original sequence of events.

Our witnessing skills, which were formerly defined more by personal opportunity and capacity than by editorial preselection, have been taken over by cameramen, reporters, and editors. They decide who is newsworthy, what should be filmed, how it should be described, and where it should go in a news program.

In addition, the program director and editor are attuned to constraints of time and budget. So they gravitate to the dramatic presentation of brief crisp copy tailored to the visual, to the quick grab for attention, hoping that the viewer or reader, thus captured, will remain captive for the commercials that interlard the news. The news of the world is snipped off into little segments subservient to the commercial message. But some forms of heroism don't fall neatly into time-limited segments; the heroic act that involves a complex sequence of events and occurs without hurrahs just isn't telegenic. It takes up too much air time without producing a wow.

Just as in the print media, women in the world of television present a contradictory picture. It's true that keen, perceptive women reporters seem to be more visible than ever. Their presence is invaluable. American audiences see and hear Lesley Stahl, Judy Woodruff, Andrea Herman, Charlayne Hunter-Gault, Elizabeth Drew, Cokie Roberts, and others reporting the news and questioning and discussing the implications. These reporters help to establish women as authentic commentators on the important doings of the world, and they represent a giant step away from the time when women reporters were limited to fashion, domestic, or "human interest" stories.

But a look at some television statistics tempers our sense of progress and presents a different and discouraging picture. Women remain seriously miscast in front of the camera and underemployed behind it. Faludi (1991) points out that the number of women news anchors and sportscasters on television fell sharply in the ten years between 1977 and 1987.

Adelson (1990) reported on a study that examined the 1989–1990 television season; 15 percent of producers were women, and women constituted only 25 percent of writers and 9 percent of directors. The study also revealed that women had fewer leading roles than men and often appeared "half-clad and half-witted, and needing to be rescued by quick thinking, fully clothed men" (1990, p. C18). In addition, in the prime-time shows on all the leading networks, women over the age of forty were rarely depicted. Faludi (1991, p. 373) reminds us of the dismissal of news anchor Christine Craft on the grounds that she was "too old, too unattractive, and not sufficiently deferential to men." In a society that promotes the new and improved version of practically everything, being passé at forty (for a woman) doesn't come as much of a surprise. But it is especially dismaying in the news room, where aging male newscasters seem to gain in authority as they gain in years. The venerable Walter Cronkite only seemed more authoritative as he grew older, but do you think Connie Chung will be broadcasting in her sixties?

Commercial Heroes

The mythology of our industrial society is dominated by the ministers of advertising. Their interests shape the media and create what Gerzon (1982, p. 233) has called a "consumer's heroism" that markets newsworthy heroes for profit. This simplistic treatment has ensured that our heroic alternatives remain limited. According to Gerzon, two types of American male heroes dominate the popular imagination: *public* heroes—the Frontiersman and the Soldier— and *private* heroes—the Breadwinner and the Expert. Commercially profitable, these "images of manhood" persist, "even though the world from which they are derived may have disappeared—if it ever existed" (1982, p. 5).

Our modern mythmakers translate the image of the hero into commercial value, attracting donations, stimulating purchases, and enlisting political support. In a nation where consumerism is next to godliness, advertisers tap the persistent human need for heroes as one more way to market their products.

Advertisers have found that the image of the hero is as profitable today as it was compelling in Homer's time. The name Medusa, for example, sells cement (an ironic adaptation of her ability to turn to stone anyone who dared look into her face), Venus sells pencils—a mysterious link there, Pegasus—in the form of a flying red horse—sells gasoline, and Atlas sells tires. Modern heroes from the fields of space, sports, and politics appear in front of us doing commercials and endorsing products. Astronauts sell cold remedies, football stars sell pantyhose, politicians sell soft drinks and credit cards—and candidates sell themselves.

Modernizing the old images, the identity mongers suggest that we can join the company of heroes by smoking a certain brand of unfiltered cigarettes—we show our contempt thereby for the sissies who fear cancer—by wearing the right shirt, having the right credit card, and using the right after-shave or deodorant. The spokesman for trucks looks like a lumberjack, the spokesman for the dependable car looks like a family man, and the spokesman for the luxury car looks like a banker or a suave man-about-town. Stereotyped images of heroism convince us to settle for the commercial identity package.

The male commercial hero, like his classic ancestor, is invincible and wide-ranging. This current representative eats real meat, summons a truck with a snap of his fingers, smokes unfiltered cigarettes, and drives a car that soars into the air or a truck that rams head-on into another equally belligerent vehicle.

What identities are offered for women?

Commercial photographers arrange idealized portraits where women pose looking docile and shy—little more than playful youngsters, indicating by an ingratiating smile and a "bashful knee bend" that they are actually in need of protection or instruction (Goffman, 1979, p. 45).

In many commercials, the underlying message is dismayingly familiar: man is the hero, and woman is either helpful, helpless, or tempting. Too many commercials present the old disturbing picture: women with little baby voices and silly smiles, blissfully contented housewives doing the laundry or polishing the tiles around the shower, seductive women who either get or are gotten by the man who uses the right product.

Women are still helpers, feeders, cleaners, and nurturers for their families. They remain back at the campsite or at home, folding their sweet-smelling laundry, nursing their photogenically sick children, or making a cup of rich, full-bodied coffee (to serve their men when *they* come in from tying up the boat against the oncoming storm).

The seller of scouring powder is a no-nonsense, energetic woman who has braved the dangers of waxy buildup on her linoleum floors; her shield is her apron, her weapon is her mop, and her mission is to disinfect the American sink and toilet. At the end of the day, however, she whips off her bandanna, unbuttons her blouse, and, with a dab of the right perfume in all the right places, becomes the seductive and available wife.

Advertising has become an efficient messenger of the latest introjected value system. The engineered perfection it promotes has become a burden to people who take these synthetic heroes seriously. Ruth came to see me because she was unhappy living a life she described as "not my own." She was the mother of two lively young children, married to a young and ambitious husband who believed in the Madison Avenue mythology about supportive mates, clean, well-behaved children, an efficiently run household—and a wife who cheerfully and charmingly feeds last minute dinner guests a gourmet meal.

Ruth was a sucker for these ideals. Trying to resolve the contradiction between her life and the advertisers' ideals was wearing her out, but she felt unjustified and disloyal in abandoning the attempt. One afternoon she spoke about the list of things-to-do she had posted on her refrigerator door. I observed that she might add to that list her responsibility to see that the sun rose as regularly scheduled. Her grin in response to my remark was a mixture of sheepishness and mischief. The next time we met she told me she had made a new sign for her refrigerator door that read: The sun will rise tomorrow even if *I* don't pull it up.

"The times," we hear, "are a 'changin.'" We see women executives in commercials on TV and husbands helping with the dishes. But listen to her tell how frozen foods make her preparation of dinner easier. The husband who helps with the dishes is grateful because the dishwashing detergent leaves his wife with lovelier hands. She's pleased because her dishes are so clean that they shine—and because her husband loves her hands. Theme and variations.

This may all seem ludicrous, but such blurred facsimiles of

real life are insidiously effective. Many people see these idyllic prototypes of masculinity and femininity, take them as true to life, try
to imitate them, and feel guilty when they fail. Nancy Mairs (1986,
p. 11) writes: "Somewhere I read that it takes the concerted pushing
and pulling of three people to get a high-fashion model zipped into
her jeans and propped into position for photographing. We all see
the photographs, though not the three laborers behind them, and
believe that the ideal woman looks like that. Thus a standard has
been fixed, and most of us, lacking the appropriate sturdy personnel, won't meet it."

Even after such strenuous preparations, the photograph can
be retouched to make it still more unrealistic. In mimicking these
images, too many of us achieve only a hollow and unstable identification that leads to the distressing suspicion that, try as we
might, we will never quite succeed. How can it be otherwise? Compared to a doctored and photogenic model of reality, ordinary folk
are bound to come out second best.

A pernicious consequence of the marketing of the ideal
woman is that the preoccupation with appearance has led to diet-
related illnesses like bulimia and anorexia. Dedicated to a model-
thin figure, some women seriously deprive their bodies. In drastic
cases, this can lead to ill health and disease. Faludi (1991) has also
noted the increasing number of women who subject themselves to
painful and sometimes life-threatening surgical interventions—like
breast implants—or skin peels, all in the pursuit of the current right
image.

Cora is one example. At twenty-two she was a professional
model for teenage fashions. Not only did she keep herself very thin
but she deliberately cultivated her adolescent appearance. One of
the ways she did this, she told me, was by making sure that when
she did her marketing, she stayed out of certain tempting aisles in
the supermarket; she went "straight to the shelves where the cottage
cheese was kept." The trouble arose when she started studying to
become a singer; her adolescent focus was sabotaging her by keeping her voice light and insubstantial, like a young girl's. To develop
a mature voice, she had to give it a mature housing. In therapy we
worked at locating her voice deeper and deeper in her body. This
involved coordinating her body with the process of breathing; she

needed to be able to produce a rich, supported voice. Somewhere Cora knew that it was time to move on from a job that required her to resist maturity. In wanting a career that required her to act her age, she was making the choice to grow up.

The advertiser's image of the aggressive, successful, beating-a-man-at-his-own-game woman can be as macho as the Marlboro cigarette man—and the cigarette in her hand is an easy prop. Look at me, she says, all dressed up and playing executive, smoking a cigarette just like the rest of the big boys. Cigarettes are symbols marketed primarily to all "junior" citizens (adolescents and women) with the same message: if you smoke this, it will make you look like the powerful people, that is, adult men. A sobering consequence is that women are now as likely to die of lung cancer as men.

Some women in commercials are lively, wisecracking side-kicks. This is one variation on the "ain't she cute?" attitude toward the assertive female who aspires to know as much as the man she's joking with—charming to the men and a sop to the women.

But to some advertisers, working women are still suspect. A commercial for a long-distance telephone company shows a busy absent father, in tune with the new male ethos, taking time off from a board meeting to softly croon birthday greetings to his daughter into the phone. When the other men around the conference table overhear him, they join him in the last chorus. Nice? This same telephone company has another commercial. Here two executive women in the fashion industry say a friendly good-bye and then each rushes into a long-distance phone booth to try to scoop the other. Energetic and independent women, it seems, are duplicitous and untrustworthy.

What is also beginning to happen is that women who have independent incomes and make independent choices are insisting that they be taken seriously. Ambitious young women are familiar with the statistics showing how few women actually do occupy executive, administrative, or other high-status positions (Hewlett, 1986; U.S. Department of Labor, 1991). Savvy women know the difference between substantial ways to catch up to their male colleagues and mere gimmicks that only make them *look* like an executive.

Some advertisers are catching on. They recognize that working women constitute a large market so they advertise in working women's magazines and financial and business periodicals (implicitly granting that women are not exclusively concerned with kitchen or nursery affairs). Some periodicals with a women's readership are refusing to run ads that they find demeaning or stereotypical. In a dramatic attempt to free itself from the tyranny of advertisers, *MS Magazine* adopted a policy of accepting *no* advertising and relying exclusively on subscriptions for revenue. But Faludi (1991) points out that this move, admirable as it was, had a downside. *MS*, with no ads, had to raise its subscription rates, and the consequence was a reduced readership. *MS*, for all intents and purposes, was purged from mainstream circulation.

Entertaining Heroes

The changing portrayal of women has been both an opportunity and a quandary for moviemakers. Some movies, to be sure, reflect the new paths that contemporary women heroes are blazing for themselves. Only a generation ago the movie *High Noon* cast the classic hero and his bride in classic roles: he the stalwart opponent of the outlaw bullies on their way to shoot him and take over his town, she the gentle pacifist who could not tolerate violence.

Recent stories about women (many of them based on fact) show them heroically fighting to keep their farms and families intact without the help of their dead or dysfunctional husbands. These women are unionizing factories to protest unsafe working conditions, exposing faulty and potentially dangerous nuclear installations, and taking to the road in boisterous adventures. Other movies are more like adult fairy tales—unrealistic and committed to the happy ending where the hardworking assistant finally gets the huge advertising contract and her man, too. The conflict that many women executives struggle with is reduced in another movie to a glib plot where a woman retires to a bucolic paradise, invents a wildly successful line of baby food, and meets a wonderful, sensitive veterinarian who is still unmarried. Nevertheless, at least these plots recognize that women may aspire to be more than secretaries, waitresses, and artists' models and that some men respect them for this.

Fictional female detectives and lawyers have followed Sherlock Holmes, Perry Mason, and the benign Miss Marple—but with significant differences. Carolyn Heilbrun (1990, p. 248) herself a pseudonymous writer of detective novels, observes that the move "away from stereotypical sex roles has found greater momentum in the detective story than in any other genre." Lively and intrepid women who don't know the first thing about cooking and housekeeping pry into villainous secrets and confront physical danger, while introspective men who are inspectors at Scotland Yard write poetry in their spare time and can whip up a gourmet meal in minutes.

Stories with women detectives describe violence less graphically. These stories deal much more with the internal experience and thought processes of the characters. Although they still have their share of murder, the female heroines do not roam the deadly landscape with a jaundiced eye and a cynical quip. For them, each death registers.

One stalwart television hero, Detective Columbo, has a wife, to be sure. But we know her only through his references to her, which are almost invariably comic. By contrast, we learn a lot about the lives of Christine Cagney and Mary Beth Lacey, two other TV detectives. We see their families; we meet Lacey's rebellious teenage son and Cagney's alcoholic father. Cagney and Lacey have indeed come a long way, baby, from "Dragnet"'s Sergeant Joe Friday and private eye Lew Archer.

Women lawyers argue their cases incisively on television and movie screens; women in business come across as being as energetic and successful as their male counterparts. Casting women in such roles has led to an unexpected humanizing development. Compare two TV shows about lawyers. In the Perry Mason stories, we never find out what his off-hours' life is like; we know only his professional life. In the tradition of the true male hero, he appears immaculately free of personal entanglements. Mason's closest relationships are with his secretary and working colleagues. A more recent program, "LA Law," showed the personal lives of both the women and the men lawyers. They are flawed: they get divorced, act unethically, and face conflicts of personal versus professional life.

Media Stew

Superficial coverage reduces an act or even a lifetime of heroism to easy slogans and shoddy image mongering. Addicts of the easy grab, we are captivated by glib facsimiles of the hero. Arranged portraits in print and film are sharp, brisk, and uncomplicated: no ambiguity, no dead air, no blank pages, no long silence, no pauses, no white space. Buzzing technology takes over, repeating and mass-producing these images, like Andy Warhol's nine identical shiny close-ups of Marilyn Monroe all on one canvas—repetition without variation, endless presentations of the same image on one newscast after another.

Such boisterous media stew confuses actual heroism with inflated mediocrity. Public figures are elevated (or reduced) to what Wilford refers to as "noisy celebrity." (1983, sec. 2, p. 1). Quiet achievement goes unremarked, obliterated in the cacophony. Pre-packaged heroism, locked into gimmickry and gesture, is heroism for the moment. Todd Christenson, tight end for the Los Angeles Raiders football team, succinctly says, "There's a big difference between celebrities and heroes. We're celebrities . . . time creates the hero. We come and go" (Greenberg, 1984, p. 27).

In presenting public heroes, the media irons out their individuality until it's hard to tell the genuine from the synthetic. The first seven astronauts, according to Wilford, were "homogenized . . . into bland Boy Scout look-alikes" (1983, sec. 2, p. 1) instead of portrayed as the distinct individuals they were. Their behavior was highlighted but also flattened out like a used up toothpaste tube, offering us a glossy surface with nothing inside. Behind the gloss, we are lead to believe, all the contents are basically the same. Just as we buy images of commodities, we buy images of heroes. The unique influence of each hero gels into slick repetitions of posture and flourish.

We need more thoughtful coverage like that provided by *Mother Jones* magazine, which yearly publishes a list of untraditional and unsung heroes, or *Newsweek* magazine, which also publishes an annual list that celebrates unsung heroes of the neighborhoods. The July 6, 1987, issue of *Newsweek* recognized women and men who commit themselves to making a difference in the *slow* events of life and who devote long hours and hard work to do it. In these lists, the names of women appear frequently. Here they are, in place day after day: Cindy Hewitt handing out meal tickets, Annie Mae Bankhead inspiring self-help efforts, Jennie Dudley cooking meals for the homeless, Ruth Prieto negotiating with South American guerrillas to obtain her mother's release, Rachel Burrell counseling the surviving children in families where a young sibling had died, Jesse White, Jr., using his experience as an athlete to set up an acrobatic program in a ghetto.

Newsweek's list of heroes shows us the cumulative image of everyday heroism, achieved bit by unpublicized bit. Beatrice Jennings and Beatrice Garvin sparked the renaissance of a run-down neighborhood in Virginia. They would ask families about to move into the neighborhood, "How would you feel about being a pioneer?" and then enlist them in cleanup and maintenance activities to make their government housing project a proud and dignified place in which to live. Betty Washington typified the eternal heroic attitude when she said, "if you get even one [drug dealer] off the street it's better than none. . . . It's important to make a difference" ("Heroes . . . ," 1987, p. 63).

These individual acts of heroism add an intimate dimension to what we have been accustomed to think of as "true" heroism. The people described in these articles are personal instances of the unmistakable humanity of heroism.

Women Writers

Unfortunately, hackneyed portrayals of women are not limited to the lively news reports of television and newspapers; the arts of biography and history haven't done much better. Women worthy of biography in their own right were either high up in the hierarchy of power—like Elizabeth I and Queen Victoria of England and Catherine of Russia—or they were people whose unlucky connections to power proved disastrous—like Mary Stuart and Marie Antoinette. The reasons for biographical attention were somewhat

bleaker for Carlotta, the tragic wife of the Mexican "emperor" Max-
imilian, and Mary Todd Lincoln, both of whom gave up on a
reality that became too painful for them. Zelda Fitzgerald struggled
frantically most of her life against obscurity in the shadow of her
husband, F. Scott Fitzgerald (Mitford, 1970).

Women writers who have wanted to explore the nature of
womanly existence in the human community in novels or in auto-
biographical writings have often labored under constrictions pecu-
liar to their sex. They have been enclosed in a psychological
architecture of home and family. Kennedy Fraser (1990, p. 116)
writes: "Women have often withheld their stories, because honesty
about emotions and about the family feels to many women like a
sin. It means drawing aside the curtains, lifting lids. It means re-
nouncing the role of good girl and ceasing to be ladylike. It may
mean expressing anger and being brave enough to watch loved ones
be angry. Women must set aside the bowl they have used to beg for
approval and praise."

But we have also been blessed by notable and heroic exceptions to these restrictions: George Eliot, disowned by her family;
Jane Austen, who wrote her subversive stories quietly in a corner
of the parlor and read them to her family; the Brontës, who first
published under masculine pseudonyms; and Emily Dickinson, the
epitome of poetic reticence. Add to these Virginia Woolf, Willa
Cather, Edith Wharton, Zora Neale Hurston. Now we have Margaret Atwood, Alice Walker, Lisa Alther, Anne Tyler, Toni Morrison, Anne Beattie, Anita Brookner, Margaret Drabble, Allison
Lurie, and so many more who are all asking the big questions: Who
am I? Who made me? What is my place in this world?

What is her place in the world, indeed? Modern society, defined by a historical uneasiness about women and power, still
doesn't know how to deal with history-making women who trespass
into male activities. The questions asked of the first woman vice
presidential candidate of a major political party, for example, often
concerned her willingness to press the button that would start an
atomic war. Nobody questioned her male opponent's willingness to
do that—nor did anybody seem to consider that reluctance might
actually be an advantage in a hostile and warlike atmosphere.

Women politicians have given reporters laughable problems

in reconciling old habits with new situations. One of the more amusing gaffes was made by a reporter who, in describing what vice presidential candidate Geraldine Ferraro was wearing, also gave her dress size. The hapless reporter quickly attempted to correct his faux pas by giving the suit size of her male opponent, George Bush, as well as describing what he was wearing.

Firsthand Heroism

It's heartening to remember the results of Farley's survey: college students and elementary school children named their parents as their heroes. (Stark, 1986.) In another article describing Farley's research in progress ("Mom and Dad . . . ," 1986, p. D1), Farley said: "People think heroes are almost overwhelmingly public people. That simply is not true. I think people view heroism occurring up close . . . as well as viewing it afar."

The young people in Farley's study suggest that before we were too influenced by the popular media and their profit-driven definitions of heroism, we recognized the everyday heroism of people close to everyday experience. We recognized the heroism that confronted concerns played on a humble stage, before a small group of witnesses. Most importantly, we honored the characteristics of an image more stable and lasting than the flickering one-dimensional media wraiths that cater to the latest marketable fads.

Conclusion

The media powerfully present and perpetuate the traditional stereotypes of the active, strong, heroic man and the gentle (read "passive") and invisibly supportive woman. Media images are so vivid and pervasive that we find it hard to set our own standards for heroism. The classic male image of heroism, dramatic and captivating, is the stuff that attracts attention and supports profit and commerce.

This kind of media coverage does not accurately reflect the state of things in the world today. It is based on the commercial and "newsworthy" priorities of the editors, who, deliberately or not, have determined that the actions, thoughts, aspirations, and enterprise of more than half of our population are not worthy of major attention.

But before prolonged exposure to the full power of these stereotypes, children understand the concept of heroism and respond to the simple but powerful heroes they know. We must recapture the ability that we, too, had as children to see the heroic in the everyday. And we must restore what we knew as children—that a fully dimensional heroism is the birthright of all women and men, not just of swashbucklers.

ELEVEN

Out of the Garden

Nothing is perhaps so wasted in our culture as the energies of its women.
　　　　　—Carolyn Heilbrun, *Hamlet's Mother and Other Women*

The role of heroism throughout the centuries has been to translate hope into actual human possibility—but always reconciling these hopes and possibilities with the social needs and dimensions of the times. *Today's* heroism must address the world *we* live in, with its own patterns of behavior and social organization. One important influence on the conduct of our times is the increasingly public contributions of women. As women have become aware of the shortcomings of contemporary institutions and policies, they have been exerting heroic efforts to make what they perceive to be necessary changes.

A key to contemporary circumstance is the need to look beyond the anachronistic mythology that sent men to the battlefields and confined women to their homes and families. The heroism of women was formed in generations of relationship, intimacy, and sustenance. This was a less flamboyant genesis, but it produced its own special wisdom, a unique and formidable perspective too valuable for our universal clan to continue to squander.

The Deadliness of Yesterday's Heroics

Many of today's women question reliance on traditional standards of heroism that revere warriorlike speed, power, and aggression.

Although it would be naive to think that these characteristics are
not crucial in many endeavors, women are increasingly unwilling
to abandon their own unique experiences with relationship, intimacy, and sustenance simply to copy male behavior.

Women do want the prestige and financial security that seem
like men's birthright, and they are willing to work as hard for them
as men do. Nevertheless, they also want their working lives to reflect
other, equally meaningful values. Linda Ellerbee, for example, describes her experience on a television program where most of the
production staff were women and where they made "coffee *and*
policy." When one woman walked in obviously distressed, "someone got that woman a cup of tea, someone gave her a squeeze,
someone said a kind word—*and then the meeting continued*" (1987,
p. 131).

Thoughtful men also recognize the risks of leaping precip-
itously into action to overcome an adversary. Mark Gerzon (1982,
p. 45) warns against stereotypical heroic leaders, calling them "yesterday's heroes." John Keegan (1987, p. 311) similarly argues that
we live in a "post-heroic" era, where leadership based on traditional
ideas of the leader-as-hero is not only inappropriate but actually
dangerous. What I propose, however, is that our era is not *posthe-
roic* but rather *neoheroic*—an age in which we need to define a new
view of heroism. Jean Baker Miller (1976, p. 88) recognizes this
historic end point when she says: "We have reached the end of the
road that is built on the set of traits held out for male identity—
advance at any cost, pay any price, drive out all competitors, and
kill them if necessary."

Today's Heroes

Neoheroism takes into account that we all live on the battlefront.
We have become accustomed to tabulations of inhuman numbers:
wartime casualties, homeless people, victims of famine and disease,
overcrowded schoolrooms, underrepresented minorities, and crush-
ing national debt. Much of the heroic work to be done today is on
untraditional battlefields against deadly enemies that invade and
threaten the most intimate aspects of human life. Women know all
about the homely details of feeding, clothing, and nursing the

young, the aged, and the infirm. Poverty, disease, hunger, ignorance, and disrespect have been the dragons that women have
battled as their adversaries.

Women, who have been poverty's primary victims, are also
the sensitive, articulate, and heroic individuals who have become
poverty's voice. Women's intimate acquaintance with human
vulnerability still reminds us, however, that tabulations of the
world's catastrophes, however large, must ultimately be divided by
one, the individual person. The objective truth is that the world is
made up of subjects.

Women's early verbal development can greatly contribute to
today's neoheroism. Women's talent with words can dramatically
increase their influence, particularly as they move this skill beyond
a diminutive and diffident vocabulary into the persuasive eloquence
that we have seen—slave or shirtwaistmaker—in times of emergency. The result of coercion is an uneasy domination. The power
of persuasion, on the other hand, is the power upon which authentic leadership rests. The pen, we have often been told, is mightier
than the sword. Let us expand that to include the spoken word, as
well as the written.

Shirley, a young social worker I know, took a courageous
stand against a discriminatory practice in the agency where she
worked. One particular group of their clients was being either in-
adequately treated or literally ignored; their claims for assistance
with medical expenses were delayed in processing, and appoint-
ments with appropriate personnel were postponed or canceled.
Knowing that whistle-blowers often get penalized in job evalua-
tions and promotions, she still protested, *in writing*, every time
another instance of this unfairness came up. Her rationale is a modern statement of the heroic position; she felt that she had to "at least,
go on record."

Today, women's voices and words inform us that effective
opportunity takes two forms: economic parity and aspirational parity. With respect to economic parity, we have seen that in primitive
communities, as well as in the neighborhoods and small towns of
more developed nations, the economic contributions of women
strongly determine the equality with which they are treated. But
equal pay for equal work implies something even greater than eco-

nomic parity. It implies that the individual's contribution (whether it is a day's work, a product, or an opinion) must also be *valued* equally. The subtleties of political argument about tariffs fade when people's main concern is to keep warm, get enough to eat, find a place to sleep, and cure disease.

Women come to these struggles with extended experience as *unofficial* authorities and activists in the arena of daily survival, but that is no longer enough. Now women are beginning to occupy *officially* authoritative positions and to exert more influence in policy-making. This is hardly an abrupt move. After all, as I have already noted, women's benevolent activities once moved them from private competence into public benevolence. The next step is for women to move in greater numbers to the administrative and political spheres, to define policy by speaking into microphones—and making sure they are heard.

But economic parity is only half the story. The other half is equal aspiration. Just as equal pay for equal work respects human life, we must recognize that women are entitled to the same aspirations for themselves—and their sisters and daughters—that men have. Women's objectives are broader than food, shelter, and clothing; they include the need for training and educational programs to alleviate deprivations at all levels of life, including the intellectual and emotional. The natural longing to carve out one's own personal style and sense of worth is no longer the exclusive preserve of male members of any given society; it is a *human* imperative.

Consuelo knew how important her aspirations were for her when she got up early in the morning, packed lunches for her children, and got her household in order before leaving for her classes. She had enrolled in a twelve-week professional training program that required her to take a two-hour bus ride each way to and from class. She had waited the years until her young children were in school all day to attend these sessions. She had vowed that she would not be trapped in one unskilled job after another. Her aspirations encompassed her daughters. She was resolved that they would have the educational opportunities she had missed, and she was willing to provide both the support and the example that had been missing in her own childhood.

Another woman whose aspirations span the generations is

Stella. Her daughter, who was in therapy with me told me about her. Stella balanced her role as a single parent with her aspirations for both herself and her daughter. After her husband died, she started a small dress store and scheduled its open hours so that other working women could shop on their time off. This schedule accomplished two things. First, Stella could attend some of the parent conferences and other activities at her daughter's school. Second, it was also a great boon for other working women who were pressed for time. After a while, Stella expanded her services by becoming a personal shopper and bringing items to the homes of women who couldn't come to her shop. Her business succeeded, and she was able to raise and educate her daughter well—and spend more time with her in the bargain. Years later, her daughter, herself financially secure, works with educationally disadvantaged children, an expanded legacy of her mother's persistence.

Other women choose a broader scope for their activities. They want to influence public policy, so they are willing to speak up in many ways. They take legal action against unfair salary and advancement practices, like Beverly Carl at SMU; they seek political office, like Pat Schroeder, Anne Williams, and Nancy Kassebaum; and they are articulate and visible commentators on political issues, like Jeane Kirkpatrick and Barbara Jordan. Women psychologists formed a political action group, Women in Psychology for Legislative Action, when they realized "that women candidates traditionally have found it more difficult to raise money, get party support and, when elected, stay in office long enough to make a difference" (Bernay, 1991, p. 6). Women in crowded inner cities call for a greater voice in the administrative decisions of their children's schools, they police the streets of their neighborhoods to free them of drug dealers, and they monitor the hallways of dirty and dangerous tenements.

More women aspire to serve in Congress, in state legislatures, on the judge's bench, in the pulpit, in combat, behind the CEO's desk, and in the university president's and dean's offices. Such women are reluctant merely to carry out programs designed by other people without their input.

Parity, both economic and aspirational, has immediate significance for women not exclusively interested in homemaker roles.

The bright, talented women who have entered various professions (law, for example) have learned—and told others—how slowly they are allowed to advance beyond associate status and how slim are their chances of becoming partners. This is no surprise. But these canny women now know that their response must move beyond simple complaint. One woman rejects what she calls useless "war stories" of inequities and emphasizes instead the importance of data and documentation as a solid base for action. (Goldstein, 1988). The documented accounts of individual women and their experiences at work can round out impersonal statistics with actual life histories.

Janis, a dedicated and ambitious attorney, decided that she was more interested in influencing the judicial system from behind the judge's bench rather than in front of it. Twelve years ago, when she came to see me, women lawyers were relatively common, but women judges were still rare. Her documentation would be the accumulation of impeccable qualifying experience. So Janis served without salary in researching material relevant to certain specific judicial decisions, pleaded numerous cases as a public service, and presided over informal adjudication sessions. This has been an exhilarating experience for her and has confirmed her dedication to become a judge.

Our legal system surely needs the corrective influence of women who challenge established legal precedent. Professor Robin West of the Law School of the University of Maryland, for example, proposes reexamining some of the assumptions that underlie legal decision making. She is particularly concerned with what she calls "gender injuries" and the legal inequities that are felt "only by women from injuries experienced only by women" (Meisol, 1988, p. V8). She provides one more voice to assert that the woman's perspective is as important in the disposition of justice as precedents almost consistently conceived and constructed by men.

Women are looking at other positions from which they have been excluded, and they are publicly protesting the too few women editors of professional journals, the low representation of women on the faculty of prestigious professional and graduate schools, and the low percentages of women appointed to federal courts or higher judicial or academic positions. Women have contributions to make in scholarly writing, in scientific research, and in determination of school policy and curriculum.

Women demanding their share of construction work (highway contracts, for example) point out that in that particular industry *they* are a minority (Johnson, 1988). Women need to better publicize the fact that they are still overwhelmingly relegated to supportive service positions in food processing, word processing, technological laboratories, and banking (U.S. Department of Labor, 1991).

As they enter business, professional, and political boardrooms, women influence the ways of doing work there. As Linda Ellerbee's experience showed, women do not have to settle for the familiar protocols by which these traditionally male organizations have long operated. Women keep score differently. They don't like the customary etiquette of boardroom conferences where male associates and partners, in the words of one unhappy stockbroker, sit around and "kick ass and take names."

Women are getting smarter politically every day. Like the women suffragists who developed their political skills in the abolitionist movement, today's women have learned valuable lessons working on other people's campaigns. Women's increased political savvy demonstrates that they *do* know how to make policy as well as coffee. Women have impact not only by designing programs based on women's priorities but also by influencing the style and the manner in which decision-making bodies work. They have the energy and persistence to exert their power and to compel compliance when persuasion fails.

It is important to remember that these women are not exclusively gentle or conciliatory. Two women who were in therapy with me described how important it was in the initial phase of their work as management consultants in the fire and police departments of large cities to establish themselves as powerful and authoritative individuals. With assertive power as additional leverage, women augment their strengths in goal setting, mutual effort, and conciliation, which are key to resolution in such areas as labor negotiations and interdepartmental relationships.

Education and Experience

Letty Cottin Pogrebin has a litmus test for her donations to women's causes, distinguishing, as she says, between "change" and

"charity." She is unwilling to "reinforce dependence." She wants
to "empower" and "enable" (1990, p. 22). Instead of being merely
a rescuer, Pogrebin aims to nourish and arouse the latent heroism
of the everyday; such inspirational effect is, remember, itself a heroic
function.

There are many enabling influences. Today it is clearer than
ever that women need two things: education and experience. Let us
enumerate how these needs can be met. Women must organize and
staff programs designed to teach illiterate *women* to read and to
develop the other skills necessary to prosper in an increasingly complex world.

We need more low-tuition or free courses in financial, man-
agerial, entrepreneurial, and administrative skills. Women who
have more time than money must support serious adult education
programs at night, when working women and mothers could attend. Too many adult classes focus on wine tasting or Chinese
cooking or the interests of already well-educated people. What
about accessible computer courses or courses in office skills? These
are too often limited to business colleges, with tuition that many
poor women cannot afford. How about some innovative solutions?
Since statistics attest that office positions are primarily filled by
women, perhaps some idealistic employer would be willing to make
office equipment available for teaching these skills to women in the
evenings, when the day's business is over. We also need a public
transportation pass to enable women to get to class. Women who
operate independent businesses must increasingly fund and staff
apprentice programs to help women start and succeed in their own
businesses.

Successful women can also speak to the women enrolled in
classes and graduate programs, answer their questions, tell them of
their own experiences and prove that other women can get there too.
They are creating their own "old girls' network" to help young
women get ahead in their careers (DePalma, 1991).

Women must promote, endow, and lobby for more student
loan funds *for women*. Furthermore, educational programs must be
accompanied by accredited child-care facilities on campuses located
in the inner city, close to public transportation. We need more
programs like the one at Jordan High School in Los Angeles, which

provides child care for its students' babies as one of the most effective ways to make sure that the young mothers finish school (Mydans, 1989). Many universities have departments that could provide student internships in campus child-care facilities or in public schools like Jordan. Education, nursing, dietetics, home economics, fine arts, social work, or psychology students could all learn by staffing such facilities under the supervision of experienced professionals and faculty.

While women's support of women is key to progress, women's self-enhancement must continue along many avenues, including political education. Study after study reveals how closely education is correlated with active political participation: the more educated the woman, the more likely she is to vote and be active in political efforts (Randall, 1982). Some standard educational subjects are also particularly valuable politically. Women need to know as much as they can about history, sociology, and political science, about policies that have already been tried, which succeeded, which failed, and why. They have to know what is politically and economically "good policy." They have to be able to argue informedly for their policies and programs, and they have to know where and to whom to present their case.

Women need more knowledge and experience in gathering, assessing, and using historical and contemporary data. They have to free themselves from the stereotype that they lack ability in mathematics and statistics. In addition to using data already available, women must generate more of their own research studies about issues important to women—and then get the results before the voters. Women need to better know how to get publicity for their efforts, how to organize like-minded supporters, and how to get financial backing for their causes.

Women's Knowledge

Another view of women that needs changing is the patronizing belief that women are more concerned with practical, rather than abstract, matters. Even John Stuart Mill, who was a passionate and eloquent supporter of women's rights, considered women to be wiser in practical thought than in matters of abstract theory. To his credit, he views this difference not as a mark of inferiority but rather as an invaluable complement to men's theoretical speculations. Benevolent as his view is, it would have been commendable if he had been able to avoid the ancient distinction between subjective and objective thinking. But he was, alas, also a product of his times. Nevertheless, he writes of the value of woman's "practical" perspective and wryly advises a man to pursue "his speculations in the companionship, and under the criticism of a really superior woman. There is nothing comparable to it for keeping his thoughts within the limits of real things, and the actual facts of nature. A woman seldom runs wild after an abstraction" ([1861] 1986, p. 64).

Mill's quaint view on women's thinking has been superceded by more rigorous and complex investigation. Belenky, Clinchy, Goldberger, and Tarule (1986) describe how a woman progresses to a full development of her own personal knowing. At the initial stage, the woman primarily learns by listening to others, who authoritatively define what is right or wrong. Soon, however, she begins to listen to her own voice and to develop greater confidence in her own opinions and reactions. Sometimes this follows her painful disillusionment with authorities whose opinions do not fit her own personal experience. Once having questioned the voice of authority, she actively works to comprehend differences of opinion, trying to understand how other people think and how their experience has affected their opinion. She puts herself in their shoes, while keeping sufficient distance to maintain her own perspective. She is absorbing the *process* of how to learn, while not conforming to the *opinion*. Finally she integrates all the sources: what authorities have said, what her own subjective experience has told her, what she has learned from other ways of thinking. She composes a personal knowledge of what fits for her—and why and how it fits. Today's woman, it seems, comes to knowledge effortfully and gradually— a far cry from Eve's quick bite from the apple.

This evolution illustrates how self-rooted knowledge for women takes a separate course from men's. As we saw in our discussion of the different social responses to little boys and girls, women emerge from a longer period of social pressure that requires them *not* to differentiate. They have undergone a learning process, formal and informal, that teaches them to be accessible, to conform, and to tend to the needs of others. Therefore, when she begins her heroic journey, each woman must extract herself from the pull of habit and custom. She must draw herself out of context, think herself out of the familiar landscape, and discover who *she* is and what *she* wants. When the barriers are formidable, this requires a heroic effort.

Leona, a patient of mine in her fifties, underwent a surpassing change of perspective. She had been reared to unthinkingly obey one set of authorities after another. She had arrived at middle age unable to confidently determine for herself the important goals in her life. At an early stage in our work together, she tried to substitute me for previous authority figures. Considering my dictatorial predecessors, I took this as an acceptable, albeit transitional, step along the way to what I hoped would be our eventual goal. Leona now reported how, when she didn't know what to do, she would ask herself what *I* would do in the same situation. Her substitution of me for the earlier figures in her life was a *stage* in her movement toward autonomy. As we continued our work together, she would tell me about some successful experiences in which she had determined her own course of action, and she would say, "You would have been proud of me." Here, though she had actually acted on her own judgment, she was still focused on my approval. One morning, Leona came in, told me how she had resolved a difficult situation, and said, "I was proud of myself." She had claimed her own authority: knowing what she wanted, acting on her own knowledge, and providing her own validation.

Some women arrive at their knowledge of self almost instinctively. They appear to spend little time in introspective thought. They are action-oriented; they move quickly into active, energetic response. Other women may respond after long periods of introspection or in concert with women who are concerned with the same purposes. Still other women respond only under great pressure, as when an accumulation of events backs them against a wall.

For example, Viola, an acquaintance of mine, had for a long time covered up the illegal and unethical behavior of her brother, who was constantly one step ahead of being jailed. In the name of family solidarity, she would plead for him, pay his fines, talk people out of taking legal action against him, and so on. Finally, one afternoon she came to the end of the line, exhausted at what this attempt had cost her. She said to me, "I'm tired of keeping the family name from public disgrace. I know I'm the only one left, but I resign." She subsequently wrote her brother, saying exactly that. This was a painful decision, but she knew it was the right one. Then, paradoxically, she turned her skills to helping others with legal troubles. In contrast to her brother, however, they really benefit from her interactions, and she feels rewarded instead of drained.

The heroic woman experiences the flux of existence; she senses the pulse of change and is hospitable to it, rather than immobilized. This ability leaves her free to create new institutions and new alliances or to find new ways of tending to human needs. Una came into therapy with me because she had gradually realized that her work was becoming more and more unpalatable. She was a respected associate in a professional firm, but she had very little voice in how the office was run. After she told me of countless staff meetings where her opinion was ignored and where she felt like an oddball, she announced that she would start her own office and run things her way. This she did, and despite the initial worry, she was elated because she could now implement her previous policies, which included a more accommodating fee scale for clients, expanded service hours, and several conveniently located offices. Four years into her new enterprise, *she* chairs the staff meetings, but with much give and take—and her associates feel influential and involved.

Women's Ways of Power

Power, like learning, is a complex and developmental ability. David McClelland (1975) observed that women and men define power differently at *different* stages in their development, and that even at the *same* stage, different individuals experience power differently. The experiential details of what is involved when women feel powerful are both illuminating and provocative. Especially fascinating are some of the parallels between the developmental stages of *knowledge* (Belenky, Clinchy, Goldberger, and Tarule, 1986) described earlier and McClelland's developmental experience of *power*.

In the first stage, power is vicarious, that is, the individual achieves it through identification or alliance with a person perceived as powerful. Men at this stage, working loose from their ties with mother, seek a male hero whose strength they can identify with or emulate. Women at this stage also identify themselves with strong men: through marriage, through service, or through mentorship. They follow in a strong man's footsteps and carry out or support his projects.

The major concern of the next stage is independence. Men, having started earlier, are farther along in their rejection of their parents, especially of their mothers, than women are. But although both women and men are concerned with autonomy, there is an important difference. According to McClelland (1975, p. 61), "the men seem concerned with *freedom from* established authority and the women with *freedom for* controlling their lives." In other words, women seem willing to acknowledge influence from outside themselves while still reserving for themselves the freedom to choose. This is reminiscent of the third developmental stage of knowledge, where the woman is interested in how other people arrived at *their* opinions but is not necessarily willing to surrender her own view.

The third stage is where power is experienced as having "impact on others." Women who experience the power to affect others show a significantly lower need for affiliation than do women at the earlier stages. Having achieved a sense of independence, however, their impact is less one-way. Their influence becomes reciprocal; they not only affect others, they are affected by them in turn. They are more at ease with themselves, so much so that they can participate as equals with others without risk to their sense of self.

The fourth and final stage is governed by the belief that the powerful woman has a concept of duty and enjoys behaving in accordance with this concept. She has an ample supply of a valuable possession, skill, or knowledge, all of which she is able to share. Through all four stages McClelland (1975, p. 75) sees a consistent trend: "Women are more concerned about having and sharing; men more about pushing ahead." This quality of sharing is especially valuable for women interested in helping other women along the road to knowledge and power.

The heroic woman's journey contrasts with the journey of

the male hero. He has been encouraged to separate early. His heroic quest, after actual physical and geographical separation, ends in knowledge (Campbell, 1973). For the female hero, the journey begins with the pressure to remain in relationship. The woman hero usually does not choose to leave her place of origin. While she may be compelled to leave through unfortunate circumstance, departure is not her traditional path. When she does choose to leave, as in several Greek legends, she often ends up unhappily. The pilgrimage of the woman hero moves through internal differentiation into self-knowledge. This frees her to inhabit and interact with her familiar world with a clearer sense of self and purpose.

Evolutionary Heroism

Much of women's heroism is evolutionary: it pivots away from an extravagant ethic of adversarial survival. Today, cooperation—in space exploration, in medical research, in collecting and distributing food, in housing and clothing the homeless and unfortunate, and in collecting and circulating information—is not only crucial to human survival but is the thriftiest way to use limited resources. Duplication of effort in a competitive race to be first is outmoded and wasteful.

The heroic struggle today is to explore and map anew the human spirit and the nature of human interaction. The quest of the heroic woman today is to redefine heroism to support and enhance life, to broaden and temper the heroic spirit so that it is relevant to everyday actions as well as to epic moments.

Many men appear ready to renounce the posturing the heroic life once seemed to require. They welcome the opportunity for a reconciliation with a side of themselves once considered alien to heroic action. They are eager for a redefinition of heroism that allows them to reincorporate the renounced parts of themselves (Bly, 1990; Keen, 1991).

Women, in their turn, have come to value the independent, outwardly directed energy that can help them reach self-defined goals. They are excited about moving to actively participate in shaping the world to their vision of what it could be. Woman's heroic journey differs from the traditional male quest because it must begin with a greater struggle to separate herself from the intense pull of home and family. Although her journey ends in union, she returns as an independent person who chooses the way she will be involved and what her contribution will be.

Conclusion

One part of the heroic quest for today's women is to be sure that, instead of helping the male hero on *his* quest, they help other women along *their* way. Their efforts to enable other women must be a dynamic combination of support, knowledge, power, and heroic energy.

Today's hero no longer has the luxury of naive exercises of power in response to simplistically identified enemies. Power and knowledge go hand in hand; indeed, they inform each other. The power of today's hero must come from knowledge, and the weapons are information, expertise, and competence.

It was inevitable that women's sense of heroism would be partly shaped by classic definitions that excluded or devalued their accomplishments. But while some women agreed to this formulation, others were creating definitions of their own, tailored to their own abilities and vision. Over the years, what was once an occasional individual female voice raised in dissent has become a chorus of women's voices telling of their heroism and calling for an expanded definition of heroism.

Epilogue

*One needs something to believe in, something for which one
can have whole-hearted enthusiasm. One needs to feel that
one's life has meaning, that one is needed in this world.*
—Hannah Senesh, quoted in *Revelations:
Diaries of Women,* edited by Mary J.
Moffat and Charlotte Painter

Brecht, in his play *Galileo* has his title character say, 'Unhappy is
the land that needs a hero." This is a reminder that some individuals and societies are immobilized by problems and hang on the
hope that someone powerful will come along and redress their
wrongs.

Brecht implies that heroism equals dependency because the
hero is the savior fantasy of the impotent. This is, of course, an
unwelcome aspect of the heroic function—one cynically employed
by many charismatic figures in history. From this perspective,
Brecht's warning has great merit. However, it is precisely because
of this possible degrading influence that we need a fresh definition
of the fundamentals of heroism. While not forgetting the dependency risks of heroism and the corrupt deformities of which it is
capable, we must also recognize that heroism is a generic human
function that we cannot blink away. It must be—in response to
Brecht—that it is not heroism that should be eliminated but the
particular poisonous forms of it that have existed for so long.

I agree with Joseph Epstein's statement (1991) that what heroes provide is a standard of idealistic endeavor. Admired, but
neither imitated nor passively awaited, they can keep alive in each
of us the possibility of courageous action. Heroes offer us a cata-

logue of the forms that human endeavors can take and from which we may invent our own heroic response.

Women now want recognition for their own heroism, vibrant but unsung in the past and luminous now. Imagine a population of heroic women, confident of their competence and of their entry into the company of those who make and implement decisions and policy. The virtues of responsibility and relatedness are preached in churches and synagogues every week, taught in ethics classes, sponsored in newspaper editorials, and envisioned in the prayers and dreams of all communally interested people. Imagine both women and men in a world where heroism is based on concerns of responsibility and relatedness.

Sometimes a goal requires a sensitive discrimination between what can be done individually in one person's life and what requires broader social change. Knowing the difference between personal action and common cause may make the difference between aggregate accomplishment or private despair.

Heroic women have made specific changes in their own lives, but they have also inspired others to join them. They have given birth to a generation of heroes that takes heart and muscle from their example and sees beyond the original visionaries. Eve had only sons, two of whom were locked into deadly rivalry. The original absence of a daughter left an opening, an entry for all the women who come after her. Daughterless as Eve may have been, every woman hero is indeed mother to those women who follow.

Parents and teachers must nurture or awaken a sense of personal continuity with their children and students. They are there in the beginning of life; they are a child's earliest heroes. Children bring color and movement to their parents' world right from birth, like the vivid swish of fingerpainting. You can sense how Anna Quindlen nourishes the heroic in her description of her two-year-old daughter: "If personalities had colors, hers would be red" (1990, p. A19). She celebrates her daughter's spirited interaction with her world, and she wants her to have that as an adult, too. The influence of a remarkable teacher can encourage children to create a vocabulary from their own experiences and write their own reading primers. And the stories they write are rich and melodramatic, way beyond Dick and Jane. They see life as full-blooded and engrossing.

Look at what Ashton-Warner calls the "private key vocabularies" of two of her Maori students. "police, butcher knife, kill, gaol (jail), hand . . . fire engine," and "Daddy, Mummy, Puki (the child's name), fight, yell, hit, crack, frightened, broom" (1963, p. 43).

In my work as a therapist, I have seen the impediments to a woman's personal sense of heroism. A woman may view her dilemma as unalterable, as requiring a course of action that she is unable, unwilling, or unready to take. She experiences no sense of choice because for one reason or another she believes herself limited to conventional or borrowed options. She has learned to define her problem in terms of inevitability, and she feels stuck. There is often an implicit double bind here. The problem, as she states it, reflects both her discontent and her fear of making (or even envisioning) the changes that might lead to a resolution because doing so risks disapproval or rejection.

Discontent or not, she may view any departure from custom as unwelcome and frightening. As frustrating as her current situation is, it is at least predictable. Her stuckness is rooted in the fact that at present she seems to prefer the known misery to the risk of unknown defeat. Her self-imposed restriction limits her to stale and inappropriate behaviors. As a result, unhappy circumstances are endured, and solution or rescue is looked for outside of herself. Sometimes she may look on the therapist as deliverer. The therapist, however, helps her to look within and invent her own solutions.

One antidote to this sense of stuckness is the awakening both of a sense of personal heroism, which honors her claim to a richer existence, and of her courage to depart from stale behaviors. As we have seen, centrally important to the heroic attitude is the willingness and ability to follow an original path, to regard oneself as the active agent in making changes, and to improvise a departure from the inadequate routine.

The process is one of *informed improvisation,* which is better than just making up something on the spur of the moment. This is improvisation based on respect for precedent but not immobilized by it. The fact that some customs have been in place for many years only means that they must be reexamined and altered to reflect contemporary need or knowledge. Once a woman has glimpsed a possible innovation, her courage to support her own originality gets a boost.

The heroic attitude of women has often improvised with what is at hand rather than undertaken a heroic "quest." All too often, a quest, rigidly defined, can become a new confinement. One woman told me, "I don't want a quest. I know how that works; you set off on a quest and when that's done, you just set another one and get started on that one." Bateson observes, "Goals too clearly defined can become blinkers" and warns against "pilgrimages to some fixed goal" (1990, p. 6).

Eve moved us all from an abundant paradise to the responsibilities and consequences of our own actions. What happened to her daring and liveliness—and knowledge—after she and Adam were expelled? Her life after Eden is dismissed in a couple of phrases describing an unimaginative and troubled life.

It is our business to see that the knowledge Eve purchased at such a high price is not wasted. Eve and her daughters have used all their ingenuity, devotion, and courage to deal with life outside of Eden. Women have defined their own unique heroism through countless quiet but life-sustaining acts. Women's heroism has persistently opposed what would diminish life, and it has been practical, rooted in the immediate and personal, and applicable to all the grand human events.

We need a new, fuller image of heroism. Let us imagine a fresh new medal struck to acknowledge today's *neoheroism*. On one side of the heroic medal is a male image—and on the other side, the image of a woman.

References

Adelson, A. "Study Attacks Women's Roles in TV." *New York Times*, Nov. 19, 1990, p. C18.

Agee, J., and Evans, W. *Let Us Now Praise Famous Men*. Boston: Houghton Mifflin, 1939.

Anderson, B. S., and Zinsser, J. P. (eds.). *A History of Their Own*. Vol. 1. New York: HarperCollins, 1988a.

Anderson, B. S., and Zinsser, J. P. (eds.). *A History of Their Own*. Vol. 2. New York: HarperCollins, 1988b.

Ashton-Warner, S. *Teacher*. New York: Simon & Schuster, 1963.

Ashton-Warner, S. *Spearpoint*. New York: Knopf, 1972.

Baer, E. D. "The Feminist Disdain for Nursing." *New York Times*, Feb. 23, 1991, p. 24.

Banta, M. *Imaging American Women: Idea and Ideals in Cultural History*. New York: Columbia University Press, 1987.

Bardwick, J. *Psychology of Women*. New York: HarperCollins, 1971.

Bartlett, J. *Familiar Quotations*. (11th ed.) Boston: Little, Brown, 1941.

Bass, A. "Assertive Women Less Influential?" *San Diego Union*, Jan. 12, 1991, p. D5.

Bateson, M. C. *Composing a Life*. New York: Penguin, 1990.

Baxter, S., and Lansing, M. *Women and Politics: The Visible Majority*. Ann Arbor: University of Michigan Press, 1983.

Becker, E. *The Denial of Death*. New York: Free Press, 1973.

Belenky, M. F., Clinchy, B. M., Goldberger, N. R., and Tarule, J. M. (eds.). *Women's Ways of Knowing*. New York: Basic Books, 1986.

Bernay, T. "Women Psychologists Urge Legislative Action" *California Psychologist*, 1991, *24*(1), p. 6.

Bettelheim, B. *The Uses of Enchantment*. New York: Random House, 1977.

Bly, R. *Iron John: A Book About Men*. Reading, Mass.: Addison-Wesley, 1990.

Buffington, P. W. "A Matter of Heroics." *Sky*, Apr. 1989, pp. 75–79.

Burke, J. *Connections*. Boston: Little, Brown, 1978.

Buss, F. L. *Dignity: Lower Income Women Tell of Their Lives and Struggles*. Ann Arbor: University of Michigan Press, 1985.

Campbell, J. *The Hero with a Thousand Faces*. Princeton, N.J.: Princeton University Press, 1973.

Campbell, J. *The Power of Myth*. New York: Doubleday, 1988.

Carlyle, T. *On Heroes, Hero-Worship, and the Heroic in History*. New York: Charles Scribner's Sons, 1903. (Originally published 1841.)

Carnegie Hero Fund Commission. *1990 Annual Report*. Pittsburgh, Pa: Carnegie Hero Fund Commission, 1990.

Cather, W. *My Antonia*. Boston: Houghton Mifflin, 1977.

Cheng, N. *Life and Death in Shanghai*. New York: Grove Press, 1986.

Chesler, P. *Women and Madness*. New York: Doubleday, 1972.

Cowan, R. S. *More Work for Mother*. New York: Basic Books, 1983.

DePalma, A. "Weaving a Network of Mentors for Young Women." *New York Times*, Sept. 11, 1991, p. B9.

DePauw, L. G. *Founding Mothers*. Boston: Houghton Mifflin, 1975.

Des Pres, T. *The Survivor*. New York: Oxford University Press, 1976.

Dinnerstein, D. *The Mermaid and the Minotaur*. New York: HarperCollins, 1976.

Dobson, R. "Theories of Myth and the Folklorist." In H. A. Murray (ed.), *Myth and Mythmaking*. New York: Braziller, 1960.

Donigian, J., and Malnati, R. *Critical Incidents in Group Therapy*. Monterey, Calif.: Brooks/Cole, 1987.

Downing, C. *Goddess*. New York: Crossroads, 1981.

Edwards, L. R. *Psyche as Hero: Female Heroism and Fictional Form*. Middletown, Conn.: Wesleyan University Press, 1984.

Eliade, M. *Myth and Reality*. New York: HarperCollins, 1975.

Ellerbee, L. *And So It Goes*. New York: Berkley Books, 1987.

Epstein, J. "Say No to Role Models." *New York Times*, Apr. 23, 1991, p. A15.

Evans, S. M. *Born for Liberty: A History of Women in America*. New York: Free Press, 1989.

Faludi, S. *Backlash*. New York: Crown, 1991.

Foderaro, L. W. "Women's Success Limited Outside Local Politics." *New York Times*, Apr. 1, 1989, p. 29.

Fraser, A. *The Weaker Vessel*. New York: Knopf, 1984.

Fraser, K. "Demented Pilgrimage." *New Yorker*, Apr. 16, 1990, p. 116.

Frazer, R. *The Golden Bough*. New York: Macmillan, 1949.

Freiberg, P. "Self-Esteem Gender Gap Widens in Adolescence." *Monitor*, Apr. 1991, p. 29.

Friedman, B. J. *A Mother's Kisses*. New York: Simon & Schuster, 1964.

Friedman, R. E. *Who Wrote the Bible?* New York: Summit, 1987.

Gerzon, M. *A Choice of Heroes*. Boston: Houghton Mifflin, 1982.

Gilbert, S. M., and Gubar, S. *The Madwoman in the Attic*. New Haven, Conn.: Yale University Press, 1979.

Gilligan, C. *In a Different Voice*. Cambridge, Mass.: Harvard University Press, 1982.

Gilligan, C., Lyons, N. P., and Hanmer, T. J. *Making Connections*. Cambridge, Mass.: Harvard University Press, 1990.

Goffman, E. *Gender Advertisements*. New York: HarperCollins, 1979.

Goldstein, T. "Women in the Law Aren't Yet Equal Partners." *New York Times*, Feb. 12, 1988, p. B7.

Goodman, E. *Turning Points*. New York: Fawcett, 1983.

Goodman, P. *Growing Up Absurd.* New York: Random House, 1956.

Graves, R. *The White Goddess.* New York: Farrar, Straus & Giroux, 1966.

Graves, R., and Patai, R. *Hebrew Myths: The Book of Genesis.* New York: McGraw-Hill, 1966.

Greenberg, A. "Todd Christensen: Los Angeles Raiders' Tight End Marches to Another Beat." *Sporting News,* Dec. 31, 1984, p. 27.

Heilbrun, C. C. *Hamlet's Mother and Other Women.* New York: Columbia University Press, 1990.

"Heroes for Hard Times." *Mother Jones,* Jan. 1988, pp. 25–33.

"Heroes, Past and Present." *Newsweek,* July 6, 1987, pp. 52–79.

Herold, L. "The Personal Battle of Beverly Carl." *Dallas Life,* Mar. 23, 1986, p. 11.

Hewlett, S. A. *A Lesser Life: The Myth of Women's Liberation in America.* New York: William Morrow, 1986.

Hilts, P. "Hero in Exposing Science Hoax Paid Dearly." *New York Times,* Mar. 22, 1991, p. 1.

Howe, I. *World of Our Fathers.* Orlando, Fla.: Harcourt Brace Jovanovich, 1976.

Huff, M. " 'Make My Day. . . .' " *American Association of Retired Persons News Bulletin,* Dec. 1988.

Hugo, V. *Les Miserables.* (C. E. Wilbour, trans.) New York: Modern Library, 1983. (Originally published 1862.)

Johnson, D. "Women and Minorities Compete for Share of Highway Contracts." *New York Times,* Mar. 5, 1988, p. 1.

Jones, A. S. "Women in Journalism Seek Place on Masthead." *New York Times,* Apr. 14, 1988, p. C32.

Josefowitz, N., and Gadon, H. *Fitting In: How to Get a Good Start in Your New Job.* Reading, Mass.: Addison-Wesley, 1988.

Keegan, J. *The Mask of Command.* New York: Viking Penguin, 1987.

Keen, S. *Fire in the Belly: On Being a Man.* New York: Bantam Books, 1991.

Keller, E. F. *Reflections on Gender and Science.* New Haven, Conn.: Yale University Press, 1985.

Kilborn, P. T. "Out of Kentucky Soil, into Their Hearts." *New York Times,* Mar. 15, 1991, p. A1.

Kornbluth, J. "The Woman Who Beat the Klan." *New York Times Magazine*, Nov. 1, 1987, p. 26.

Lefkowitz, M. *Women in Greek Myth*. Baltimore, Md.: Johns Hopkins University Press, 1986.

Lerner, G. *The Majority Finds Its Past: Placing Women in History*. New York: Oxford University Press, 1979.

Luchetti, C. *Women of the West*. St. George, Utah: Antelope Island Press, 1982.

McClelland, D. C. *Power: The Inner Experience*. New York: Irvington, 1975.

McGrath, R. D. "Daniel Boone's Empire." *New York Times Book Review*, May 5, 1985, p. 14.

McLuhan, M. *The Mechanical Bride*. Boston: Beacon Press, 1967.

Mairs, N. *Plaintext*. New York: HarperCollins, 1986.

Malcolm, A. H. "Giving a Dose of Empathy to the Dying." *New York Times*, July 5, 1991, p. A12.

Martin, M. K., and Voorhies, B. *Female of the Species*. New York: Columbia University Press, 1975.

Maynard, J. "Updates on the Rug, Adultery and Other '87 Issues." *San Diego Union*, Dec. 26, 1987, p. D6.

Meisol, P. "A New Genre of Legal Scholarship." *Los Angeles Times*, Oct. 7, 1988, p. V8.

Mill, J. S. *The Subjection of Women*. New York: Prometheus Books, 1986. (Originally published 1861.)

Miller, J. B. *Toward a New Psychology of Women*. Boston: Beacon Press, 1976.

Milton, J. *Paradise Lost*. New York: Odyssey Press, 1935. (Originally published 1667.)

Mitford, N. *Zelda*. New York: HarperCollins, 1970.

Moers, E. *Literary Women*. New York: Doubleday, 1976.

Moffat, M. J., and Painter, C. (eds.). *Revelations: Diaries of Women*. New York: Random House, 1975.

"Mom and Dad No. 1 in Hero Department." *San Diego Tribune*, June 23, 1986, p. D1.

Monaghan, P. *The Book of Goddesses and Heroines*. New York: Dutton, 1981.

Montagu, M. W. *Essays and Poems and Simplicity, a Comedy*. (R.

Halsband and I. Grundy, eds.) Oxford: Clarendon Press, 1977. (Originally published 1803.)

Murray, H. *Myth and Mythmaking*. New York: George Braziller, 1960.

Mydans, S. "School Offers Day Care for Teen-Age Mothers." *New York Times*, Dec. 27, 1989, p. A14.

Nadelson, C. C. "Women Leaders: Achievement and Power." In R. A. Nemiroff and C. A. Colarusso (eds.), *New Dimensions of Adult Development*. New York: Basic Books, 1990.

Nye, P. "Women Elected Officials Make Substantial Gains in State Governments." *National Voter*, Oct./Nov. 1990, p. 12.

Oates, W. J., and Murphy, C. T. *Greek Literature in Translation*. White Plains, N.Y.: Longman, 1944.

Ochs, C. *Behind the Sex of God*. Boston: Beacon Press, 1977.

Ostriker, A. S. *Stealing the Language*. Boston: Beacon Press, 1986.

Pagels, E. *The Gnostic Gospels*. New York: Random House, 1979.

Pagels, E. *Adam, Eve and the Serpent*. New York: Random House, 1988.

Phillips, J. A. *Eve: The History of an Idea*. San Francisco: Harper-Collins, 1984.

Pogrebin, L. C. "Contributing to the Cause." *New York Times Magazine*, Apr. 22, 1990, p. 22.

Polster, E., and Polster, M. *Gestalt Therapy Integrated: Contours of Theory & Practice*. New York: Random House, 1973.

Pomeroy, S. B. *Goddesses, Whores, Wives, and Slaves*. New York: Schocken Books, 1975.

Quindlen, A. "The Glass Half Empty." *New York Times*, Nov. 22, 1990, p. A19.

Randall, V. *Women and Politics*. New York: St. Martin's Press, 1982.

Rank, O. *The Myth of the Birth of the Hero*. New York: Random House, 1959.

Redl, F. "Group Emotional Leadership." *Psychiatry*, 1942, 5, 573–596.

Reese, L., Wilkinson, J., and Koppelman, S. *I'm on My Way Running*. New York: Discus/Avon, 1983.

Rich, A. *On Lies, Secrets, and Silence*. New York: W.W. Norton, 1979.

Rimer, S. "At Bronx School, She 'Holds It All Together.'" *New York Times*, Apr. 5, 1990, p. A1.

Rossi, P. H. "The Old Homeless and the New Homeless in Historical Perspective." *American Psychologist*, Aug. 1990, pp. 954–959.

Rubin, L. B. *Women of a Certain Age*. New York: HarperCollins, 1979.

Sarton, M. *A Private Mythology: New Poems*. New York: W.W. Norton, 1966.

Saywell, S. *Women in War*. New York: Viking Penguin, 1985.

Senesh, H. "Hanna Senesh." In M. J. Moffat and C. Painter (eds.), *Revelations: Diaries of Women*. New York: Random House, 1975.

Shaevitz, M. H. *The Superwoman Syndrome*. New York: Warner Books, 1984.

Shaw, E. "Can We Rename Nature?" *New York Times Book Review*, Apr. 28, 1985, p. 36.

Shipp, E. R. "'Patron Saint of Civil Rights' Lends Her Weight to Voter Drive." *New York Times*, Jan. 24, 1988, p. 20.

Stark, E. "Mom and Dad: The Great American Heroes." *Psychology Today*, May 1986, p. 12.

Stephenson, J. *Women's Roots*. Napa, Calif.: Diemer-Smith, 1986.

Stone, M. *When God Was a Woman*. Orlando, Fla.: Harcourt Brace Jovanovich, 1976.

Tannen, D. *You Just Don't Understand*. New York: William Morrow, 1990.

Tavris, C. *Anger*. New York: Simon & Schuster, 1982.

Thurber, J. *The Thurber Carnival*. New York: HarperCollins, 1945.

Turkington, C. "Farm Women and Stress." *Monitor*, June 1986, p. 18.

Ullyot, J. *Women's Running*. Mountain View, Calif.: World, 1976.

U.S. Department of Labor. Bureau of Labor Statistics. *Employment and Earnings, 1990 Annual Averages*. Washington, D.C.: U.S. Government Printing Office, 1991.

Vare, E. A., and Ptacek, G. *Mothers of Invention*. New York: William Morrow, 1988.

Walker, B. *The Woman's Encyclopedia of Myths and Secrets*. New York: HarperCollins, 1983.

Warner, M. *Joan of Arc: The Image of Female Heroism.* New York: Random House, 1982.

Warner, M. *Monuments and Maidens.* New York: Atheneum, 1985.

Weiss, P. "Whistlegate." *Mirabella,* June 1991, p. 99.

Wilford, J. N. " 'The Right Stuff': From Space to the Screen." *New York Times,* Oct. 10, 1983, sec. 2, p. 1.

Williams, J. *Psychology of Women.* (3rd. ed.) New York: W.W. Norton, 1987.

Winerip, M. "Grannies Keep Crack Dealers at Bay." *San Diego Union,* Nov. 27, 1988, p. D5.

Wolf, C. *Cassandra.* New York: Farrar, Straus & Giroux, 1984.

Wollstonecraft, M. *A Vindication of the Rights of Woman.* New York: W.W. Norton, 1975. (Originally published 1792.)

"Women Gain in State Posts." *New York Times,* Jan. 23, 1988, p. S1.

"Women Scientists Find Barriers in Jobs." *San Diego Tribune,* Dec. 26, 1985, p. AA1.

World Book Encyclopedia. Chicago: Field Enterprises Educational, 1960.

Wylie, P. *Generation of Vipers.* New York: Pocket Books, 1959.

Zeig, J. (ed.). *The Evolution of Psychotherapy.* New York: Brunner/ Mazel, 1992.

Name Index

Subject Index

and pedestal, 107–108; restrictive, 118–119; sexual, as divine law, 114; of spirit, 123, 144–146; and sports, 112–113; terrain of, 105–112; women's limited access to, 108–112; writings on, 112–116

Georgia, initiative in action in, 27

Germany, childbearing in, 127. *See also* Nazi concentration camps

Glen Cove, New York, grandmothers in, 137

Grandmothers, as heroic, 10–11, 137, 144

H

Hardship, and geography of heroism, 119–123

Heroes: caretakers of, 140–143; celebrities distinct from, 46, 162; characteristics of, 22–31, 46, 106; commercial, 155–160; courage of, 27–30; current, 168–173; entertaining, 160–162; faith in effectiveness by, 24–26; and family separations, 129–130; images of, 9–10, 185; imperfect, 149–150; life respected by, 23–24; lifelong search for, 44–49; naming, 42–43; need for, 7; nonviolent, 18, 33; old views of, 12–15; original perspective of, 26–27; population of, 21–41; public or unpublic, 30–31, 118; in televised news, 153–155

Heroines. *See* Heroes; Women heroes

Heroism: attributes of, 7–9, 21–22; balanced sense of, 6, 8, 20; caricature of, 17; characteristics of, 22–31, 46, 106; and choice, 127–128; concepts of, 9–11; conclusions on, 5–6, 20, 41, 182–185; and creation myths, 1–6; deadliness of yesterday's, 167–168; and dependency, 182; disquieting, 139–151; enlarged view of, 21–41; entitlement to, 42–56; first-

hand, 165; functions of, 50–54; future for, 167–181; geography of, 104–123; legacy of concepts of, 7–20; male-skewed, 7–9, 17, 54–55; and necessity, 87–103; new views of, 18–19; outdated views of, 15–18; pace of, 55–56; practical, 102; proper and improper, 13–15; and socialization, 42–86; and technology, 16; unpublic, 30–31, 118; villainy related to, 76

Homemaking, and gender differences, 61–62, 67–68

Horticultural communities, women's roles in, 92–95

I

Improvisation, informed, 184–185

Industrial communities, women's roles in, 100–103

Infants: environmental interactions of, 15; gender differences in, 57–58

Initiatory magic, and courage, 29

Innocence: aspects of socialization in, 70–86; gender differences for, 71–77; as ideal, 5; imposed, 74–76; outgrown, 86

Islam, and pastoralist communities, 96

Italy, heroic geography in, 111

J

Jefferson Medical College, and woman applicant, 29

Jordan High School, child care at, 174–175

K

Kentucky, clinic in, 120

Kinship. *See* Family ties

Knowledge: aspects of socialization in, 70–86; background on, 70–71; choice and responsibility related to, 79–85; conclusion on, 85–86;